MW00745643

HAPPY BIRTHDAY,
PRINCESS

24 YEARS YOUNG
↓
WELCOME TO MIDLIFE!

I LOVE YOU, KATE
IN MIDLIFE AND
BEYOND!

Your

Jonathan
xxx...

MIDLIFE

MIDLIFE

Eugene Stickland

broadview drama

NATIONAL LIBRARY OF CANADA CATALOGUING IN PUBLICATIONS DATA

Stickland, Eugene, 1956-
   Midlife
   (Broadview drama)
   A play.
   ISBN 1-55111-498-4

   I. Title. II. Series.

PS8587.T534M52 2002   C812'.54   C2002-900004-1

PR9199.3.S797M52 2002

~

BROADVIEW PRESS LTD.
is an independent, international publishing house, incorporated in 1985.

Canada	*United Kingdom*
Post Office Box 1243	Thomas Lyster Ltd.
Peterborough, Ontario	Units 3 and 4a, Old Boundary Way,
Canada K9J 7H5	Burscough Road, Ormskirk
Tel: (705) 743-8990	UK L39 2YW
Fax: (705) 743-8353	Tel: (01695) 575112; Fax: (01695) 570120
customerservice@broadviewpress.com	books@tlyster.co.uk

U.S.A.	*Australia*
3576 California Road	St. Clair Press
Orchard Park, NY 14127 USA	Post Office Box 287
Tel: (705) 743-8990	Rozelle, NSW 2039
Fax: (705) 743-8353	Tel: (02) 9818-1942l
customerservice@broadviewpress.com	Fax (02) 9418-1923

www.broadviewpress.com

Broadview Press gratefully acknowledges the financial support of the Ministry of Canadian Heritage through the Book Publishing Industry Development Program.

~

Book design by Lori Shyba, Sundial Media Ltd.
Cover photography by Brian Harder for Trudie Lee Photography Inc.

Printed in Canada
by McAra Printing, Calgary, Alberta

For Bernie

ACKNOWLEDGEMENTS

MIDLIFE *was workshopped at the 2001 Banff Colony —*
a partnership between the Canada Council, the Banff
Centre and Alberta Theatre Projects; the author gratefully
acknowledges the support of the Canada Council for the
Arts. Thanks also to Maureen Labonté and the National
Theatre School of Canada, especially the students in the
playwriting program; Paula Danckert and Playwrights
Workshop Montreal; Bradley Moss and Theatre Network,
Edmonton; the staff of Alberta Theatre Projects, in
particular the play development team of Vanessa Porteous,
Vicki Stroich and Bob White; Lori Shyba for a beautiful
and thoughtful design; and a special thanks to all the
actors who have read the play in developmental workshops
along the way. Finally, thanks as usual to Carrie and
Hannah.

INTRODUCTION

M IDLIFE is the fifth play I've written for Alberta Theatre Projects, the fourth since I began my term as Playwright in Residence for the company in 1994. The plays I've written for ATP have followed a two year cycle. A production of a play marks the end of the cycle for a particular play, and the beginning of the cycle for the new one. Because the PanCanadian *playRites* Festival ends in March, by May or June I have usually regrouped and steeled my resolve to begin a new one.

Around the time I was starting to write this play, I had an interesting conversation with my dramaturg and director Bob White about the phenomenon of the easy and immediate — one might say cheap — intimacy that can be found on the Internet, compared to the much more difficult and complex process of being engaged in a meaningful human relationship. We talked about the nature of human relationships, and the difficulty in maintaining them. And we talked about the way our views and priorities, and our wants and desires, change as we grow older, as we grow up.

In many ways, that's what this play set out to be — a dramatic exploration of some of the themes and ideas that Bob and I touched on in our conversation. Some of these, I suppose, can still be found in the play but there comes a point in the writing process that the characters take over the direction of the script and the play becomes what they will have it become. On the surface of things, looking at the text now, it seems that very little is left of what Bob and I originally discussed.

There have been other major changes that occurred over the

development of the play. I began the actual writing of *Midlife* while I was a resident playwright at the National Theatre School in Montreal in the fall of 2000. I suppose being in a new environment and having the luxury of time to explore the themes and ideas Bob and I had discussed led to a lot of what one might call "interesting" writing. I call the writing generated at this stage of the process "prewriting," an important, even essential step to make, but I doubt that very much of the writing I did in Montreal is actually present in this volume.

With a few inciting ideas floating around, and thousands of handwritten words that had something to do with the concept of midlife, I was somewhat flummoxed as to how to proceed. This prompted the creation of an outline — the first time I'd ever tried such a thing. The outline was conceived along very formulaic lines. I decided I would write the play for four characters. It would be a two act play, each act consisting of four sections, with each of these sections comprised of four scenes. The play, in that version, began with the characters sitting in chairs, speaking to the audience (if not to the audience, at least not to one another), and this convention was repeated every four scenes.

This turned out to be a pretty good idea, on paper at least. And having such a formal blueprint helped me get the first draft written. Bob and I returned to Montreal with an edited version of that draft, and heard the play read at the NTS with actors from Playwrights Workshop Montreal, a strange sort of tri-pro between ATP, NTS and PWM. A few things were discovered at this reading. Because the play, in my mind at least, is obviously set in Calgary, I had been worried it might not translate to a Montreal audience — albeit a small audience of NTS students, all originally from somewhere other than Montreal. Yet it seemed to carry quite well.

The other discovery was that the character of Jack's wife, Darlene — the fourth character in those early drafts — wasn't all that interesting, dramatically. Never one to be precious about such things, I cut her scenes, and replaced them with the monologues that Jack now has throughout the play. In a strange way, Darlene is more present and interesting now than when she was actually in the play. This decision, of course, utterly destroyed my neat little formula based on fours, and we then decided that the play was not in fact a quartet, but a trio. But by this time, it didn't really matter. The characters were aching to get on with their story and there was no longer any need for a formula to get them there. It had served its purpose, and it was time for me to let go.

Midlife was presented as a Platform Play at ATP's PanCanadian *playRites* 2001. The draft we presented there was about draft five, I believe. I subsequently had the opportunity to work on the play at the Banff PlayRites Colony. There I began what I called the eight series, which included three drafts. I returned to Calgary and started the nine series — two more drafts leading to the Rehearsal draft, which changed drastically as we prepared the play for its premier production. I guess all in all, *Midlife* went through some 12 or 13 drafts, before it was finally distilled into its present form. For anyone interested, all of these drafts will eventually end up in my archival collection at the University of Regina.

Eugene Stickland
Calgary
January 16, 2002

Midlife was first produced by Alberta Theatre Projects as part of PanCanadian *playRites* 2002, with the following cast:

DELVECCHIO ...... Kevin Kruchkywich
JACK .... Ric Reid
AMBER .... Daniela Vlaskalic

SET DESIGNER .... Scott Reid
COSTUME DESIGNER .... Dave Boechler
LIGHTING DESIGNER .... Melinda Sutton
COMPOSER/SOUND DESIGNER ...... Kevin McGugan
FESTIVAL DRAMATURGE .... Vanessa Porteous
ASSISTANT DRAMATURGE .... Vicki Stroich
PRODUCTION STAGE MANAGER ..... Dianne Goodman
STAGE MANAGER .... Crystal Beatty
ASSISTANT STAGE MANAGER .... Karen Fleury
UNIVERSITY OF CALGARY INTERN ... Angela Bewick

Eugene Stickland gratefully acknowledges the support of:

Le Conseil des Arts du Canada | The Canada Council for the Arts

THE BANFF CENTRE
FOR THE ARTS

CHARACTERS

JACK PALMER
An executive in an oil company, 50-ish.

JOHNNY DELVECCHIO
A Landman in the same company, under Jack's supervision, 30-ish.

AMBER O'LEARY
An employee of the oil company, 20-ish.

SETTING

As is apparent, for the most part, the action of the play takes place in the offices of a large oil company. Given that Midlife *received its premiere production at Alberta Theatre Projects, on the thrust stage, it was impossible to depict the setting in any realistic fashion. Thus I have dispensed with the usual stage directions indicating setting, and I invite directors and designers to be as naturalistic, or abstract, as they choose.*

ACT ONE

~

ONE   *THE DROP ZONE*

JACK: I'm starting to worry, as I lie in bed at night, sleeplessly watching the minutes and hours tumble by, that I'm basically falling apart at the seams . . .

DELVECCHIO: I am 6 foot 4 inches tall. 200 pounds. Cut. Curly blond hair. Dazzling blue eyes, like little flakes of the prairie sky…

AMBER: OK. So this is good. I think. Yeah. Sure it is. This is going to be good. I can do this. I can work in a place like this…

JACK: Lying awake in the dark, feeling the various stabs of pain leap-frogging across my limbs and organs … The throat cancer. The lung cancer. The neck cancer. The shoulder cancer. The inter-rib cartilage cancer. The brain cancer. The brain tumour. The aneurism.

DELVECCHIO: I am 6 feet even. 190 pounds. Lean and elegant. I have long black hair, so shiny that it shines blue. Like Superman. Like Reggie Mantle. I have green eyes, like shattered emeralds in snow.

AMBER: It's going to be great. It's like … Oil! No great mystery there. Oil's good. Show it in a good light. That's all they want me to do. Show it in a good light. I can do that. For what they're paying me, I can show oil in any light they want …

JACK: Lying in our darkened room, listening to the steady rhythm of Darlene's breathing, staring into the dark space above the bed, and these pains settle on my chest and push their fingers deep and hard into the soft hole around my heart, filling me with dread and speculation of my demise. No doubt about it. I am in the Drop Zone.

DELVECCHIO: I am wearing an Armani suit. I look good in it. It's like Armani had me in mind when he designed this thing. Oh! And burgundy silk boxers. I like the feeling of silk against my skin. Do you? Do you like the feeling of silk against your skin? So tell me, what are you wearing?

AMBER: The thing I don't get, is the dress code thing. Maybe I spent too long at university. I just don't get it. Like, I'm reading newsletters. Who cares what I'm wearing? Anyway, I can't just sit here all day. First step: find the supply cabinet. Grab some pens, and a notebook, then I can get down to some serious work … . After my coffee break, of course …

∾

TWO   *WACKING*

JACK, holding a driver.

JACK: You know, it's getting harder and harder to get a game of golf in. Like this morning. She's sitting in the kitchen drinking a cup of coffee, staring out at the back yard. She says there's all these weeds and crab grass out by the back fence and it's driving her to distraction. You see what she's like. She allows crab grass to drive her to distraction. So I say, why don't you get what's his name — Juan — to get out there and wack it? That's what we pay him for. She tells me he has an issue with the weed whacker. That's how she talks: he has an issue with the weed whacker. So I say, he's a gardener. How can he have an issue with a weed whacker? Well, apparently he was attacked by one. At least, by an assailant who was armed with one. I'm supposed to feel sorry for this kid. I'm supposed to get out there and wack the weeds myself while he sits on my deck drinking lemonade. Not only that. She thinks I should get to know him better. She thinks he thinks I don't like him. Well, they're both right about that. I don't like him. She says, Oh but he's a lovely young man. I say, I know, I don't like lovely young men. She asks why? That's a no-brainer. I don't like them because they're lovely. And they're young …. And so I try to tell her about my dream of getting out here enough this year, with my head reasonably clear of mundane stuff like weed whackers and lovely young men, so I at least have a chance — a chance — of breaking 90. She has no idea. She starts taking issue. She puts her foot down. The weeds and the crab grass are driving her to distraction and she wants me to stay at home and wack 'em. She wants me to give up my golf game so I can stay at home and wack the crab grass. Un-believable. Finally, I say, Honey, there's a certain type of man who might forego his golf game and stay home and attend to the crab grass. We call that man a pussy-whipped man, and I am not that man. See ya later. You can see what I have to go through, just to get in a simple game of golf.

$\sim$

THREE   *WHIPPED*

DELVECCHIO: I am five foot ten. 130 pounds. I am sixteen years old. I think of only one thing, and I think of it all the time. I'm a hot, hard electrical wire looking for someone to connect with —

JACK: Delvecchio!

DELVECCHIO: Yeah, Jack?

JACK: Can I see you for a minute?

DELVECCHIO: Sure. What's up?

JACK: A few things.

DELVECCHIO: OK.

JACK: How you been?

DELVECCHIO: Been good.

JACK:	Good.
DELVECCHIO:	You?
JACK:	Yeah. Been good.
DELVECCHIO:	Good. How's Darlene?
JACK:	She's great.
DELVECCHIO:	She's a great lady.
JACK:	Yeah. She sure is.
DELVECCHIO:	A great lady.
JACK:	She sure is.
DELVECCHIO:	You're a lucky guy, Jack.
JACK:	I sure am.
DELVECCHIO:	You'll have to say hi to her for me.
JACK:	I sure will.
DELVECCHIO:	For sure.
JACK:	For sure. So you been out yet?
DELVECCHIO:	No.
JACK:	No?
DELVECCHIO:	Not yet.
JACK:	No, eh?
DELVECCHIO:	No. Haven't even got the clubs out.
JACK:	Serious?
DELVECCHIO:	I've been going through some stuff …
JACK:	Right.
DELVECCHIO:	Just haven't found the time. You been out?
JACK:	Yeah.
DELVECCHIO:	That's good.
JACK:	Yeah. Been out four times now? Five? Four or five?
DELVECCHIO:	Who with?
JACK:	Kelly, a couple of times.
DELVECCHIO:	How was that?
JACK:	Well, you know how it is, golfing with your brother-in-law. I suspect he shaves a few strokes here and there.

DELVECCHIO:	No doubt. So how'd you shoot?
JACK:	Don't ask.
DELVECCHIO:	Well, it's early.
JACK:	Yeah. Problem is, I took some lessons when Darlene and I were down in San Diego this winter. I think I told you about that trip we took down there?
DELVECCHIO:	Oh yeah ...
JACK:	Yeah. I took some lessons while I was down there and these lessons have ruined my game. Utterly ruined my game. Now I step up, all I hear is the voices. Chin in. Head down. Left arm straight. Knees bent. Hands loose. Hands tight. Relax. Don't relax. Eye on the ball. I can't remember. All I know is that because of these lessons I took, my game is hooped.
DELVECCHIO:	Lessons are bad.
JACK:	Utterly hooped.
DELVECCHIO:	You'll get it back.
JACK:	Yeah. I just need to forget what I learned and I'll be OK.

Slight pause.

JACK:	So ... how's work been going?
DELVECCHIO:	Good.
JACK:	Yeah? How are your contracts coming along?
DELVECCHIO:	OK. More or less.
JACK:	Getting back in the swing of things?
DELVECCHIO:	I think so.
JACK:	How's the Horton thing coming along?
DELVECCHIO:	The Horton thing?
JACK:	Yeah. You know. The Horton thing?
DELVECCHIO:	Well, Jeez. The Horton thing. What can I tell you?
JACK:	I don't know. That's why I'm asking.
DELVECCHIO:	Well, actually it's coming along a bit slow, eh?
JACK:	Oh yeah?

DELVECCHIO: Yeah. Real slow, actually.

JACK: I see.

DELVECCHIO: Yeah.

JACK: So, why is it so slow?

DELVECCHIO: Well, I don't know. There are certain factors, I guess.

JACK: Factors?

DELVECCHIO: That's right.

JACK: What kind of factors?

DELVECCHIO: Mitigating factors.

JACK: Like what?

DELVECCHIO: Well. It's like: I'm OK with the guy. You know?

JACK: Horton.

DELVECCHIO: Yeah. Horton. I'm OK with Horton. You know?

JACK: OK …

DELVECCHIO: The seat of the problem is it's not Horton himself who's calling the shots out there.

JACK: Oh?

DELVECCHIO: The problem is that this Horton dude is one of those chinless watery-eyed types who's basically whipped beyond all human measure.

JACK: Oh?

DELVECCHIO: Yeah. I've never seen anything like it. And making matters worse, his wife is one of those wild back to the land organic types. Hemp shirts. Timothy Findley books lying around all over the place. Ranting and raving about the environment. She doesn't care for us so much. She doesn't care for our industry. She absolutely can't stand the sight of me.

JACK: Right.

DELVECCHIO: Plus: if that weren't enough, she's got a gun, eh?

JACK: Really?

DELVECCHIO: Oh yeah. A big gun. Shotgun. Some great big over-under thing.

JACK: Remington or something.

DELVECCHIO: Something like that. Remington. Winchester. Some great big over-under thing.

JACK: Well …

DELVECCHIO: I know.

JACK: Shit.

DELVECCHIO: Tell me about it.

JACK: You know what it is?

DELVECCHIO: What?

JACK: It's the women these days, eh?

DELVECCHIO: Yeah. The women …

JACK: Yeah … the women … . Wild, shotgun-toting women, out of control and their husbands too whipped to tell 'em to put it down. To just say: Put the gun down.

DELVECCHIO: That's what it is, all right.

JACK: I don't know what's happening to this world. I don't know what's happening to the men of this world. You know? The men of this world. What's happening to them?

DELVECCHIO: They're all whipped.

JACK: Yeah. Every last one of them.

DELVECCHIO: Yeah.

JACK: Except us of course …

DELVECCHIO: Right. That goes without saying.

JACK: Absolutely.

DELVECCHIO: I have to tell you something, Jack. I'm not planning on ending up like Ullman.

JACK: No.

DELVECCHIO: No way.

JACK: No, we can't have that.

DELVECCHIO: I don't want to end up dead on some hillbilly's front porch like Ullman. Shot in the fucking back. And that was the wife that shot Ullman.

JACK: I know.

DELVECCHIO: And her whipped husband just stood there and watched the whole thing go down. Watched her shoot him, the poor fucking bastard, and he had like ten kids or something.

JACK: He had two kids.

DELVECCHIO: Still.

JACK: And he was separated.

DELVECCHIO: Whatever. All I'm saying is I like the job and stuff. I like being a Landman. It's who I am. And I'm glad I came over here and I like it here but I'm not taking a bullet in the back like poor old Ullman.

Slight pause.

JACK: OK. So those are the factors.

DELVECCHIO: The mitigating factors.

JACK: Right. The need to get access mitigated by the crazy wife with the big gun. So, what are you going to do about it? What's your plan of action?

DELVECCHIO: Well, I guess I've got to suck it up and get back out there.

JACK: Yeah. That's a good start.

DELVECCHIO: I don't know. I'll call. If it doesn't seem to be going anywhere I'll get the RCMP, I guess.

JACK: Absolutely. You're not going in alone. Not with her being armed and everything.

DELVECCHIO: No way.

JACK: But you do have to go. You have to go back. Right?

DELVECCHIO: Right …

JACK: And not next week either. I need you to get on this right away. I have to take a meeting with Kelly and the boys upstairs. The first thing they're going to ask is what's happening with that property. I have to be able to tell them we're all over it. OK?

DELVECCHIO: OK.

JACK: All I'm asking is for you to do your job.

DELVECCHIO: Right.

JACK:	That's why we pay you. To do your job.
DELVECCHIO:	Yeah, I know.
JACK:	I know it's been a tough time for you, lately. That kind of shit, you know, that shit that you've been going through, with what'shername —
DELVECCHIO:	Sharon —
JACK:	Sharon. Right. But you have to keep moving forward. You know?
DELVECCHIO:	Yep.
JACK:	Yeah. And that's what work is good for sometimes, Delvecchio. It helps you forget how shitty the rest of your life is. You get in, in the morning. You have a coffee. You read the paper. You change your outgoing message to reflect the dawning of the new work day. Suddenly you have a purpose. You know?
DELVECCHIO:	Yep.
JACK:	That's why the Horton thing is so very important. Critical, even. Not just to the company — of course, it's important to the company — but it's important to you. To your life. You know?
DELVECCHIO:	Yep.
JACK:	Yeah?
DELVECCHIO:	Yep.
JACK:	Good stuff.
DELVECCHIO:	Yep.
JACK:	OK. That's all. Now, I don't want to have to tell you this again.
DELVECCHIO:	Right …
JACK:	Let me know how it works out.
DELVECCHIO:	Right …

~

FOUR   *KEEPING TABS*

JACK: I don't know … These young guys these days, think the world owes them a living or something. You've got to get down on your knees and beg them to do a day's work. Man, when I started out, all I had was a pocket full of dimes for the pay phone and a cast iron stomach for all the well-water coffee the farmers would throw down your throat. Oh, and a pair of binoculars to keep tabs on what the other guys were up to … . Yessirree, Bob … those were the days … .

~

FIVE   *THE NEW GAL*

        AMBER, *with a bottle of designer water, is reading a film magazine.* DELVECCHIO, *with a cup of coffee, approaches her. After sending out a million signs and getting no response, finally* DELVECCHIO *can restrain himself no longer.*

DELVECCHIO: Excuse me …?

AMBER: Yes?

DELVECCHIO: I was just wondering something.

AMBER: Yes?

DELVECCHIO: Sagittarius?

AMBER: I beg your pardon?

DELVECCHIO: Your sign? Of the Zodiac? Sagittarius?

AMBER: No.

DELVECCHIO: Oh …

AMBER: Not at all, actually.

DELVECCHIO: Right. Me neither.

Slight pause. She reads.

DELVECCHIO: So …

AMBER: Hmmm?

DELVECCHIO: See that hail last night?

AMBER: No.

DELVECCHIO: You didn't see that hail?

AMBER: No.

DELVECCHIO: Wow. That's amazing you missed it. That was some hail. Big suckers. Like golf balls, eh?

AMBER: I'm sorry. I guess I missed it.

DELVECCHIO: Too bad. It was pretty wild.

AMBER: Sounds wild.

DELVECCHIO: It was. It was wild. Pretty wild. Like, for weather. Or whatever …

Slight pause. She reads.

DELVECCHIO: So you're the new gal, I assume …

AMBER: The new gal?

DELVECCHIO: Yeah.

AMBER: The new gal?

DELVECCHIO: Yeah.

AMBER: Is that what they call me? The new gal?

DELVECCHIO: Yeah.

AMBER: I didn't know anyone still used that word.

DELVECCHIO: Around here they do.

AMBER: Right …

DELVECCHIO: Why? Are you a strident feminist or something?

AMBER: No … not really. Are you?

DELVECCHIO: No. I don't think so.

AMBER: Why?

DELVECCHIO: 'Cause of the gal thing.

AMBER: No. I just think it's a geeky kind of word.

DELVECCHIO: Oh. Right. Me too …

Slight pause. She flips through the pages.

DELVECCHIO: Say … .

AMBER: Yes?

DELVECCHIO: Do you like movies?

AMBER: I like films.

DELVECCHIO: There's a difference?

AMBER: An aesthetic one. Don't you think?

DELVECCHIO: I don't know. I just like going to movies. Something to do. Whatever.

AMBER: Right. It's probably just semantics when you get right down to it.

DELVECCHIO: Right … You seem to know a lot about it. Movies. Films. Whatever.

AMBER: I've got a degree in film studies.

DELVECCHIO: Cool. So what are you doing working at an oil company?

AMBER: I don't know. I've got a million dollars in student loans. I needed something that pays. Plus: I have an uncle who works here. He kinda helped me get in.

DELVECCHIO: Oh yeah. Who's that?

AMBER: Martin Berry?

DELVECCHIO: Serious? Martin Berry's your uncle?

AMBER: Yeah.

DELVECCHIO: How's that thing with his nose?

AMBER: Well, they've stopped it from spreading.

DELVECCHIO: That's good.

AMBER: Yeah, everyone in the family's really happy about it.

DELVECCHIO: No doubt … So, where do they have you working?

AMBER: Public Affairs.

DELVECCHIO: Oh yeah? You making a movie or something? A film?

AMBER: Well, they've got me working on the newsletter. For now. But I'm supposed to be making a video, actually. Eventually.

DELVECCHIO: A video about what? About this place?

AMBER: Yeah.

DELVECCHIO: Far out. Hey!

AMBER: Yes?

DELVECCHIO: Well, if you need any actors or whatever. You know? I have a bit of experience.

AMBER: Oh yeah?

DELVECCHIO: Yeah.

AMBER: Like what?

DELVECCHIO: Well, I played the letter "C" in our Christmas pageant, back in grade three.

AMBER: I see. I'll keep that in mind.

DELVECCHIO: Great.

AMBER: Yeah.

DELVECCHIO: So, I'm a Landman.

AMBER: What's that?

DELVECCHIO: What's a Landman?

AMBER: Yeah.

DELVECCHIO: You work at an oil company and you don't know what a Landman is?

AMBER: Not really.

DELVECCHIO: Oh. OK. Well, I guess you could say I'm a negotiator. I do all the deals around here. I'm kinda one part lawyer, one part farmer, and one part used car salesman.

AMBER: I see.

DELVECCHIO: Heart and soul of the oil patch. Right here.

AMBER: Cool.

Slight pause.

DELVECCHIO: So, anyways … my name's Johnny. Johnny Delvecchio. For some reason, everyone around here calls me Delvecchio all the time. Maybe they're all so amazed there's an Italian Landman out there. Like I think I'm the only one. I don't know. But I don't mind. About the name thing. Like, it's my name. So I don't mind. So. What's your name?

AMBER: Amber.

DELVECCHIO: Amber. That's nice.

AMBER: Thanks.

DELVECCHIO: You're welcome. Amber. *(Under his breath)* Amber Amber Amber Amber Amber Amber —

AMBER: What are you doing?

DELVECCHIO: That's how I remember names. Say them seven times. Amber. There. That's seven.

Slight pause.

DELVECCHIO: So, are you married, or anything like that? Amber? Got a boyfriend, or anything like that?

AMBER: No.

DELVECCHIO: Yeah, same here. Well. I was. Till a couple of weeks ago. I had a girlfriend, I guess you'd call it. Partner. Whatever. We were living together. Condo. Nice carpet — green shag. Balcony. Dishwasher. But she went behind my back a few times, eh?

AMBER: That's too bad.

DELVECCHIO: Yeah. In fact, I'm starting to find out that she was screwing half the landmen in the patch. Not that I'm the jealous kind. People get drunk, I guess. People screw people they don't know. Indiscriminately. Whatever. Accidentally. I don't know. You see it happen. Well, not the actual — you know. You see the lead up. You know? Not the foreplay or whatever. How could you? But the preamble. You know? I don't know. I might sound old-fashioned, but I can't help wonder what's happening in the world today. Like. Where are our values? Hmmm?

AMBER: I don't know.

DELVECCHIO: Like, there should be trust, don't you think?

AMBER: Yes.

DELVECCHIO: Hey?

AMBER: Absolutely.

DELVECCHIO: Yeah. Trust. If nothing else. There should be trust …
Yeah. So anyway. You know. It just. Yeah. Anyway. Sorry.
Where did that come from?

AMBER: I don't know.

DELVECCHIO: Sorry.

AMBER: It's nothing to be sorry about.

DELVECCHIO: Right.

AMBER: It's OK. Anyway, I guess I just had my fifteen minutes… .

She starts to leave.

DELVECCHIO: Right. Well, maybe we'll see each other around and stuff.

AMBER: Probably.

DELVECCHIO: Hey! Listen.

AMBER: Yes?

DELVECCHIO: Well, I was — Well. Assuming we manage to hit it off or
whatever. I thought. A movie. Film. Film. You know.
Maybe. A film some night. You and me. Whatever. What
do you think?

AMBER: Are you asking me out?

DELVECCHIO: Yeah, kinda, I guess.

AMBER: Hmmm.

DELVECCHIO: So what do you think?

AMBER: I don't know.

DELVECCHIO: No?

AMBER: I'm not sure.

DELVECCHIO: Oh.

AMBER: Like, is it allowed?

DELVECCHIO: What?

AMBER: Dating.

DELVECCHIO: What do you mean, allowed?

AMBER: Like company policy, or whatever?

DELVECCHIO: Oh, believe me. Around this place, it's pretty much a given. Yep. For some of us more than others …

AMBER: I had a professor at university. He was a great guy. He looked like Einstein, with the white hair and all that, you know? He was amazing. And he used to say, "If your grandmother had a mustache, would that mean she was your grandfather?" You know?

DELVECCHIO: Kinda.

AMBER: Yeah?

DELVECCHIO: Yeah.

AMBER: This is a bit like that, don't you think?

DELVECCHIO: Yeah.

AMBER: That's cool.

DELVECCHIO: Yeah.

AMBER: I'm glad you're able to grab onto something like that. A lot of guys these days just don't seem to get it.

DELVECCHIO: Right. Great! Well. That's great. That's cool. OK, then. Well. Gee. I guess I'd better get back at 'er I guess.

AMBER: OK.

DELVECCHIO: Couple of fires to put out. You know?

AMBER: OK.

DELVECCHIO: Nice talking to you.

AMBER: You too.

DELVECCHIO: Bye.

AMBER: Bye.

~

SIX   *THE GOLF*

JACK, holding a low iron.

JACK: OK. Chin in. Head down. Left arm straight. Knees bent.

Hands loose. Hands tight. Relax. Don't relax. Eye on the ball. God. Voices. How do you stop the voices? *(He stops and walks away from the ball.)* OK. Yeah, so anyway, right. Now we're having a bit of a fight. Mostly being fought out in silence. The things not said. But it's like, you know, dishes shoved into the dishwasher with a little too much velocity. Or vigour. Gusto. Whatever. Something's up. But nothing's said. So you watch *Law & Order*. You've seen it. But you watch it. Again. You go to bed. In your flannel pyjamas. The absence of desire. The lack of need. Whatever. Lack lack lack. And I feel her hand on my back as I lie there and I know how simple it would be to turn back into her and let's face it, it would do us both some good. But I lie there, silently, fighting back the realization that this isn't working out for either of us, yet we're locked into it somehow, and to stay is just so much easier than doing something about it. Simpler. And it's not like there's anyone else. I mean, there's everyone else. But no one else. Just lying there in the silence and the unspoken dread that things will always be just as they are at this moment, unchanging, unrelenting, till death do us part … . And suddenly she props herself up on one elbow and leans over and whispers in my ear: "I think it's the golf." The golf. The golf? What the hell are you talking about, the golf? She says, "The golf is driving a wedge between us." I tell her I don't want to talk about it. "Why?" Because golf is sacred. Holy. Sacrosanct. I like that. Sacrosanct. So she tells me about this article she read, about the attitude of the average middle-aged guy toward the game of golf. I of course reminded her I'm neither average nor middle-aged. She said as if. Which I thought was uncalled for. Anyway, according to Darlene, the idea behind this stupid article is that at a certain age, men give up on sex and spend all their time and energy on golf instead. To which I asked, So what's your point? That didn't go down so well. That led to the serious fight. And now to resolve it, nothing will do but we're going to have a date. An actual date. I don't get it. We're married. Why would we want to go out on a date … ?

∼

SEVEN   *MIND YOUR P's AND Q's*

DELVECCHIO: I am Or-ham, Prince of the Dark Dwelling Places beneath the mountains, and connoisseur of fine lingerie. Those who would know Me must learn to submit to My iron will.

JACK approaches DELVECCHIO.

They must come to Me on their knees, wearing only the finest silk and lace -——

JACK: Delvecchio?

DELVECCHIO: Jack!

JACK: What the hell are you doing?

DELVECCHIO: Nothing. Just summarizing some reports. You know? Blazing the old paper trail —

JACK: Yeah, well never mind that. I've been up to see Lindsay.

DELVECCHIO: Oh yeah …

JACK: Yeah.

DELVECCHIO: How was that?

JACK: Well … you know …

DELVECCHIO: How was Lindsay?

JACK: Silent, as usual.

DELVECCHIO: What else is new? What about Kelly? Was Kelly there?

JACK: Kelly was there.

DELVECCHIO: What kind of mood was Kelly in?

JACK: Basically, the mood is not good up there, Delvecchio. The mood is not good.

DELVECCHIO: How can the mood not be good? I don't understand how it's possible for the mood to not be good. The price is holding. It's through the roof. Like for over a year now. The stock's performing. Development coming out of the ying yang. How can the mood not be good?

JACK: Because things are going too good.

DELVECCHIO: You're saying the mood's not good up there 'cause things are going too good?

JACK: They're all nervous up there. That's the thing about profit, Delvecchio. If you're truly driven by it, then it's never enough. They're like back alley junkies up there, crazy for their next fix. And there's never enough for them.

DELVECCHIO: So what are they doing up there?

JACK: What else? Downsizing.

DELVECCHIO: Are you shitting me?

JACK: No.

DELVECCHIO: Downsizing?!

JACK: Yes.

DELVECCHIO: Record profits and they're downsizing?!

JACK: It's like I say: they're junkies.

DELVECCHIO: I'll say.

JACK: Never enough.

DELVECCHIO: Bastards.

JACK: I know.

DELVECCHIO: So, who are they downsizing?

JACK: I can't say.

DELVECCHIO: Anyone I know?

JACK: I can't —

DELVECCHIO: Come on, Jack. Did you hear any names?

JACK: Yeah …

DELVECCHIO: Anyone I know?

JACK: Between us?

DELVECCHIO: Yeah.

JACK: Doesn't leave this room?

DELVECCHIO: Between us.

JACK: OK. Well, the name I heard was Sawchuck.

DELVECCHIO: Sawchuck?!

JACK: Yeah.

DELVECCHIO: Are you serious?

JACK: Yeah.

DELVECCHIO: Sawchuck?!

JACK: Sawchuck.

DELVECCHIO: Why Sawchuck?

JACK: I don't know. Why not Sawchuck?

DELVECCHIO: He's got fucking kids, for one thing. Four kids or something like that.

JACK: One kid.

DELVECCHIO: Still.

JACK: One kid grown up, moved out.

DELVECCHIO: Whatever. It's not like the old days when you could just walk across the street after lunch and find something better for yourself. It's getting tight out there. Poor bastard. Poor fucking bastard …

JACK: Well …

DELVECCHIO: Poor fucking bastard, a kid and everything …

JACK: Delvecchio?

DELVECCHIO: Yeah?

JACK: Get a grip. Sawchuck's a millionaire about twenty times over. He'll make more from his severance than my father made in his entire life.

DELVECCHIO: Yeah, well still …

JACK: On top of that, everyone knew he was in the bag by two in the afternoon, every afternoon. He wasn't performing. He's gone. So let it go, OK?

DELVECCHIO: Yeah … Still — OK …

Slight pause.

DELVECCHIO: You never really liked Sawchuck all that much, did you Jack?

JACK: Aw, for crying out loud —

DELVECCHIO: I mean, he's from your floor and you couldn't even protect him?

JACK: Listen: someone had to go. It was him.

DELVECCHIO: At least we could have a lunch for him or something. Don't you think? Some kind of cake or something?

JACK: I don't know. He's gone. Let it go, will you?

DELVECCHIO: OK. Man … . I wonder what he'll do with his time …

JACK: I don't know.

DELVECCHIO: Does he golf?

JACK: I don't think so.

DELVECCHIO: Then what does he do?

JACK: I think he's into gardening.

DELVECCHIO: Gardening?! Jeez. What kind of lame, idiotic waste of time is gardening?!

JACK: I know. I don't know.

DELVECCHIO: Why wouldn't he golf?

JACK: I don't know.

DELVECCHIO: Poor Sawchuck. Poor sorry bastard …

JACK: The thing is, Delvecchio, that's the prevailing mood upstairs. Today it's Sawchuck. Tomorrow, it could be anyone. Anyone. You understand?

DELVECCHIO: Yeah.

JACK: So you make sure you mind your p's and q's. Make sure you've dotted all the i's and crossed the t's on your contracts. And you can start with the Horton thing. Because I mean it, they're getting very nutty up there, and if they decide to come down on you, and they will if this isn't done toot de sweet, then you're really going to have troubles. Major. There won't be much I can do to help.

DELVECCHIO: Right.

JACK: Just make sure. Things can't stay this good much longer. Once it starts to settle down, once things start getting bad again, everyone will take a deep breath and we can all relax a little —

AMBER *approaches* JACK *and* DELVECCHIO.

AMBER: Excuse me? Oh. Hi.

DELVECCHIO: Hi! Amber.

AMBER: Right. It's you. Sorry. I was looking for the supply cupboard. Like, the main one? Is there a main one?

DELVECCHIO: Oh, yeah.

AMBER: I was hoping so. Like, I found this lame kinda little cabinet thing by my office with a few broken pencils in it and those balls, you know, those old typewriter balls, that's all it had in it. I was just looking for some notebooks or whatever. If it's OK if I take them, like no one's really come by to explain all of that to me. But I was thinking like some notebooks and a new pen might be kind of nice, you know?

DELVECCHIO: Oh. Well. Right. The main deal's up on the next floor, actually. I could probably show you the ropes, hook you up with some supplies.

AMBER: Great!

DELVECCHIO: There was a lot of shrinkage in that department so they decided to centralize it. There's a few forms to fill out but I can help you get through them.

AMBER: Thank you.

DELVECCHIO: No problem. Oh. Amber, this is Jack. Jack, this is Amber. Amber's the new gal.

AMBER: Hi.

JACK: Hi. So you're the new gal …

AMBER: I guess so. Jack Palmer, right?

JACK: Yes.

AMBER: I recognize you.

JACK: You do?

AMBER: I saw your picture in the newsletter. You're in there a lot.

JACK: Well, I've been kicking around this place for a long time.

AMBER: I'll say. You're kind of a pioneer.

JACK: I know. I feel like it some days.

AMBER:	You won the golf tournament or something, last year didn't you? I think that's why your picture was in there…
DELVECCHIO:	No one really wins the golf tournament …
JACK:	I got longest drive.
AMBER:	Oh.
JACK:	I got lucky and caught a good one.
AMBER:	That's cool. And you also do the food bank thing?
JACK:	Yeah. I try to get some people around here to dig in and help out. Some of them have deep pockets and short arms, but we made a nice donation last year.
AMBER:	I wouldn't mind contributing to that. This year.
JACK:	Great.
DELVECCHIO:	Yeah, I think I gave you twenty bucks for that last year, didn't I, Jack? Twenty or thirty?
JACK:	Actually, you gave five.
DELVECCHIO:	Oh? I thought it was at least twenty.
JACK:	Five. *(To AMBER)* How do you know about all this company lore and legend?
AMBER:	I just read every newsletter ever printed in this place. Twice.
JACK:	That must have been a moving experience.
AMBER:	Oh, yeah. Anyway. Sorry to interrupt. Guess I'll find the next floor.
DELVECCHIO:	I'll show you.
AMBER:	Oh. OK. *(To JACK)* Nice meeting you, Mr. Palmer.
JACK:	Call me Jack.
AMBER:	OK, Jack. Nice meeting you.
JACK:	Yeah. You too.
AMBER:	*(Offering her arm to DELVECCHIO)* Shall we?
DELVECCHIO:	For sure … .

They walk away, arm in arm.

~

EIGHT   *HOPE*

JACK: That was interesting ...

DELVECCHIO: Man oh man. . .

AMBER: Well he's certainly got it all going on ... .

JACK: Very interesting ...

DELVECCHIO: Man oh man oh man. She gave me her arm!

AMBER: The last thing I was expecting to find, but how do you
               know what's around the corner ... or who ...

JACK: The way she looked at me ...

DELVECCHIO: And the way she looked at me ...

AMBER: Interesting, the way he looked at me ...

JACK: Or am I just imagining things ... ?

DELVECCHIO: And the way she took my arm. The way she said, Shall
               we? Shall we? I like that. Shall we?

AMBER: Strange. Hmmm. The older man thing. You hear about it.
               You see them, out there. In the bar. On the street.
               Driving. Whatever. Maybe there's something to it ... .

DELVECCHIO: And what did I say? For sure. Oh man, that's lame. Shall
               we? For sure. Jeez. That's really lame.

AMBER: Well you got the look from land boy there ...

JACK: But why would she want to look at me like that?

DELVECCHIO: Still, there can be no doubt about it ...

AMBER: But I just got the look from Jack Palmer ...

JACK: Twenty years ago, maybe ... .

AMBER: That could be a whole different ball game ...

DELVECCHIO: Yessirree, Johnny boy, you studly boy you ...

JACK: I'm almost old enough to be her father ...

AMBER: He's probably old enough to be my father ...

JACK: She called me Mr. Palmer, for Christ's sake ...

DELVECCHIO: The long dry spell may be over at last ...

AMBER:	But for whatever reason …
JACK:	Yet there was something kind of charming about that …
AMBER:	And for whatever reason it doesn't matter …
JACK:	It doesn't matter …
DELVECCHIO:	Clearly she was saying yes in the coffee room … .
AMBER:	But on the other hand, what'll it look like?
JACK:	What am I saying?
DELVECCHIO:	And I say this: Let the healing begin …
AMBER:	Who cares what it'll look like?
JACK:	Of course it matters.
DELVECCHIO:	It's just a matter of time till you'll be riding high in the saddle once again …
JACK:	I'm probably just imagining the whole thing anyway …
AMBER:	Who cares? You can't live your life, worrying about what other people think …

~

NINE *BABOSITY*

JACK , with a fairly sophisticated lunch system: the insulated bag; plastic containers for veggies, sandwiches, a piece of pie, etc.; a thermos for soup. He opens one of the containers and takes out half a sandwich. He finds a note, obviously from his wife.

JACK: Right. A date. A date. Hmm. A date with my wife, no less. I was never very good at it when I had to be. I'm an engineer. What do I know about dating? It was a big relief to get married and not have to bother with it anymore. The last time we dated, I bought her a wrist corsage, for Christ's sake …

DELVECCHIO approaches JACK. He opens a Coke.

DELVECCHIO: Well?

JACK: Well what?

DELVECCHIO: What did you think?

JACK: About what?

DELVECCHIO: Amber.

JACK: Who?

DELVECCHIO: Amber.

JACK: Oh. Right. The new gal.

DELVECCHIO: Yeah. So what did you think?

JACK: She seemed OK.

DELVECCHIO: Just OK?

JACK: I don't know.

DELVECCHIO: She's more than just OK, Jack.

JACK: I suppose.

DELVECCHIO: Christ, Jack. What's wrong with you? She's a major hottie. Big time, downtown, all around, Hot-tie.

JACK: "Hottie?"

DELVECCHIO: Well, yeah.

JACK: Is that the expression nowadays? Hottie?

DELVECCHIO: Yeah. And that's just part of it. It's not just her general babosity, not that there needs to be anything beyond that, but she's smart, too eh?

JACK: Really?

DELVECCHIO: Oh yeah. Like she's some kind of film director or some such.

JACK: Really?

DELVECCHIO: Yeah.

JACK: What's she doing working for an oil company?

DELVECCHIO: She's Martin Berry's niece or something.

JACK: Oh yeah?

DELVECCHIO: Yeah.

JACK: What's happening with his nose?

DELVECCHIO: I don't know. She seems to think it's getting better. Anyway, they've got her in Public Affairs. She's going to be making a film. About us.

JACK: Oh yeah?

DELVECCHIO: Well, a video.

JACK: Another one of those corporate things.

DELVECCHIO: Yeah.

JACK: Showing us all in a good light.

DELVECCHIO: Yeah. And get this: I'm going to be in it.

JACK: Isn't that nice?

DELVECCHIO: Yeah. So what do you think?

JACK: About what?

DELVECCHIO: Her. And me.

JACK: I don't know. Why? Are you dating her or something?

DELVECCHIO: Yeah. Well. More or less.

JACK: You asked her out?

DELVECCHIO: Yeah.

JACK: And she said yes?

DELVECCHIO: Well, I'm not sure what she said actually. But it wasn't "no." And if it wasn't "no," it must have been some form of "yes." Right?

JACK: I wouldn't know.

DELVECCHIO: It's only a matter of time. I've laid the table. Won't be long now till I'm sitting down tucking into the feast.

JACK: Well.

DELVECCHIO: So, what do you think?

JACK: She seemed nice. And, clearly, a hottie and everything, I guess. But I don't know …

DELVECCHIO: What?

JACK: She's a tad young for you, don't you think?

DELVECCHIO: You think?

JACK: She can't be very old.

DELVECCHIO: She's old enough.

JACK: She seems kind of young. Kind of innocent or something.

DELVECCHIO: She can buy smokes. That's old enough for me.

JACK: Yeah, she's still young. I can't imagine what she'd see in an older guy. She probably has all kinds of offers from boys her own age.

DELVECCHIO: I'm not that much older than her. And I really don't think she's too young, Jack. Like, she may be youthful, chronologically speaking. But she's an old soul. You can see it in her eyes. A very old soul.

JACK: I don't know. It's probably none of my business. I guess. Probably. But you know what they say ...

DELVECCHIO: No. What do they say?

JACK: Well, with her being Marty Berry's niece and everything, I'd just be careful about dipping your nib in the company ink well.

DELVECCHIO: What the hell does that mean?

JACK: It means like don't shit in your nest.

DELVECCHIO: I'm not shitting in my nest.

JACK: I'm just saying be careful.

DELVECCHIO: I know what I'm doing. I'm not shitting in my nest.

JACK: OK ...

DELVECCHIO: I know all about shitting in my nest and this is not shitting in my nest, OK?

JACK: OK. Whatever. And by the way ...

DELVECCHIO: Yeah?

JACK: I'm sorry to have to bring this up because I know you're busy and everything, and I know it can be inconvenient when work interferes with your social life ...

DELVECCHIO: What?

JACK: Just if it's not too much trouble, you know ... if it's not too distracting for you, perhaps you could look into the Horton situation? You know. The thing you're actually getting paid to do around here?

DELVECCHIO:	Oh. Right.
JACK:	Yeah. I'm not going to be able to hold Kelly off forever on this thing.
DELVECCHIO:	I'm all over it.
JACK:	You better be.

DELVECCHIO moves away.

JACK:	What do I know about it anyway? I'm still dating my wife…

JACK goes back to his lunch.

~

TEN   *TONIGHT'S JAPAN*

AMBER approaches JACK.

AMBER:	This may be right out of the blue.
JACK:	Yes?
AMBER:	And it may sound a tad forward.
JACK:	OK …
AMBER:	I hope you don't mind.
JACK:	I don't think so.
AMBER:	Right. Good. OK. I was wondering …
JACK:	Yes?
AMBER:	Well, just if you thought you could get away this evening… .
JACK:	I can get away anytime I like.
AMBER:	Really?
JACK:	Yes. Some men can. Some men can't. I'm one of the men who can.
AMBER:	That's cool.

JACK:	Right. So?
AMBER:	Right. Well, down at Broccoli tonight?
JACK:	Broccoli?
AMBER:	Yeah. Broccoli. Do you know it?
JACK:	I know broccoli the vegetable. I don't really care for it. But you're thinking of something else, I'd imagine.
AMBER:	Yeah. I'm thinking of, like, the club?
JACK:	The club Broccoli.
AMBER:	Down on 1st?
JACK:	Right. Of course.
AMBER:	You know it?
JACK:	Well, I haven't actually been there. Yet. But it's something I've always wanted to do. To get down. There …
AMBER:	It's a really cool place. It's kinda anti-club, you know?
JACK:	I'm not sure.
AMBER:	Well, anyway, they're having this film series … ?
JACK:	Yes?
AMBER:	International avant garde cinema?
JACK:	Right.
AMBER:	Tonight's Japan.
JACK:	Ahhh. A film from Japan?
AMBER:	Yeah.
JACK:	An avant garde film from Japan?
AMBER:	Yeah. OK. I know. You think Japanese cinema, you're thinking Kurosawa, right?
JACK:	It goes without saying.
AMBER:	Well, there's a whole new generation of Japanese film makers out there. And they're absolutely amazing.
JACK:	I'm sure they are.
AMBER:	This film tonight, for example?
JACK:	Yes?
AMBER:	It's like five hours long!

JACK:	Oh?!
AMBER:	And get this: there's like only six lines of dialogue.
JACK:	Six lines in five hours?
AMBER:	Yes. It's very avant garde.
JACK:	I'll say ...
AMBER:	So, what do you think?
JACK:	About what?
AMBER:	About going?
JACK:	Going to Broccoli?
AMBER:	To see the film.
JACK:	Just you and me?
AMBER:	Just you and me.
JACK:	Tonight.
AMBER:	Yes.
JACK:	I see ... Well, isn't that something?
AMBER:	So?
JACK:	There's just one little problem ...
AMBER:	Yeah? What's that?
JACK:	Well it's just that I'm — uhh — how would you say? .... kinda married?
AMBER:	Kinda married?
JACK:	That's right.
AMBER:	Oh shit. Really?
JACK:	Yeah. Kinda.
AMBER:	Oh God. I'm so sorry. Really. What an idiot. God. Really, you are?
JACK:	Yeah.
AMBER:	Oh my. Oh, Jesus. I can't believe. I'm just so bloody. You know? Impetuous. I drive myself crazy. I'm always doing stuff like this. Always. What's wrong with me?
JACK:	It's OK. Really, it's OK.

AMBER:	No, it's not OK. I'm always jumping in and making a fool of myself and it's like my first day and already I'm screwing everything up. God.
JACK:	You're being a little hard on yourself, there, uh -—
AMBER:	Amber.
JACK:	Sorry. Amber. *(He touches her in a comforting way.)* You're being a little hard on yourself.
AMBER:	I don't think I am.
JACK:	No. Really. It's not that bad. In some places, it would be quite natural.
AMBER:	Oh yeah?
JACK:	Yeah.
AMBER:	Like where?
JACK:	I don't know. Paris?
AMBER:	That's a long ways away.
JACK:	Well, not just Paris. Parts of Montreal. It happens all the time. And Montreal's in Canada. More or less. So you're not too far off the mark.
AMBER:	Really?
JACK:	Really. It's OK.

> *Slight pause. Suddenly, they are aware that they are touching.*

JACK:	It's only on tonight?
AMBER:	Tomorrow's Turkey.
JACK:	I see. It all sounds very exciting. But to tell you the truth, I have a bit of an engagement tonight.
AMBER:	I see.
JACK:	Yeah.
AMBER:	What?
JACK:	What what?
AMBER:	What are you doing?
JACK:	Oh. Well. Actually, I have a — golf game. A game of golf. Yeah. I'm golfing. Actually.

AMBER:	At night?
JACK:	Yes.
AMBER:	I see.
JACK:	I don't get out much … .

She breaks away from their touch.

AMBER:	That's too bad.
JACK:	Yes.
AMBER:	'Cause I was thinking, you know …
JACK:	Yes?
AMBER:	Well, maybe after the film we could go back to my place for a while. You know? Talk about the film? Maybe hang out a bit? Drink some tea? I have the place to myself. Like, my mom's not home. You know?
JACK:	Your mom?!
AMBER:	Yeah. I live with my mom.
JACK:	I see. What about your dad?
AMBER:	Daddy died a few years ago.
JACK:	Did he really?
AMBER:	Yeah. He was just getting out of the shower. And he dropped. Just like that. Big strong guy in the prime of his life. Bang. Cut to black. You know?
JACK:	Oh yeah. I know.
AMBER:	Well, he lived his life. I don't think he had any regrets. Anyway. I don't want to put you on the spot. Whatever you feel better doing, I guess. I understand that for some people, golf is kinda sacred. Like, especially for men of a certain age.

Slight pause.

JACK:	Broccoli, eh?
AMBER:	Yes.
JACK:	Five hours.
AMBER:	Yes. Six lines of dialogue. It starts at seven.

JACK:	OK.
AMBER:	Really?
JACK:	Yeah. I'll see you there.
AMBER:	Serious?
JACK:	Yes.
AMBER:	Cool.
JACK:	I'll see you there a bit before. We'll get some popcorn or whatever.
AMBER:	Far out.
JACK:	Yes. It certainly is far out …

⁓

ELEVEN *DREAD*

JACK: Oh boy … oh boy …. What the hell was that? Trouble and madness, that's what that was. This is not good. This is not good at all. Man. What was I thinking, saying yes? As if I'm going back to her place. For tea. Tea? I don't drink tea. And then what? Get naked with her? That's a very scary thought. Like, I'm going to suddenly get buff in the next couple of hours, is that what I was thinking? There's no way. There's just no possible way. God. This is not good. What the hell was her — ? Amber. Christ. That's not the name of anyone I've ever gone out with. I'm supposed to be going out on a date with my wife. What did I just say yes to? Oh boy. This is deviation from the routine, big time. This is not good. No way. I can't go. I'll go home, like a good boy. But God help me, who knows if a chance like this will ever come 'round again? I'll go. No, I can't go. I have to go. God. I don't know. I just don't know …

∼

TWELVE *FEAR*

JACK approaches DELVECCHIO.

JACK: Why are you here?

DELVECCHIO: Why am I here?

JACK: That's what I'm asking you.

DELVECCHIO: Well, gee, I don't know. Why are any of us here?

JACK: Why are you here in town? At the office? That's what I'm asking you, Delvecchio. Why aren't you out taking care of the Horton thing?

DELVECCHIO: I just had to sort out a few details, then I'm outta here.

JACK: You're sorting out the details here?!

DELVECCHIO: Yeah.

JACK: Why?

DELVECCHIO: This is my office, Jack.

JACK: So?!

DELVECCHIO: So that's what I do here.

JACK: You have a notebook computer. A Palm Pilot. A cell phone. A fax machine in your car. You're wired and you're mobile. And I need you out there, Delvecchio. You're no good to me here. You're no good to anybody here. I didn't hire you to sit on your ass all day. I need you to get out there, and get that whipped son of a bitch's signature on that contract or I can't guarantee what's going to happen to you around here. OK?

DELVECCHIO: OK.

JACK: OK. So let's get on it.

DELVECCHIO: Right.

JACK: You can call the RCMP from your car.

DELVECCHIO: OK.

JACK: Have them meet you out there.

DELVECCHIO: Right.

JACK: Get his signature on the contract and then get your ass back here.

DELVECCHIO: Right.

JACK: Let me know the minute you get back.

DELVECCHIO: Right.

JACK: Bring the contract directly to me.

DELVECCHIO: Right.

JACK: You can go now.

DELVECCHIO: Yeah.

JACK: I want you to go now.

DELVECCHIO: OK.

JACK: Now!

DELVECCHIO: OK.

JACK: Get the hell outta here!

DELVECCHIO: She's armed, Jack.

JACK: Oh for Christ's sake —

DELVECCHIO: She's armed and they're like twenty miles from the nearest town and they've got these huge dogs that want to rip you apart the minute you get out of your car and her eyes are all rolled back into the back of her head and she's spouting scripture and waving that big gun of hers around and that whipped husband standing there like a zombie dribbling Copenhagen down his chin, looking at me like he's thinking of cutting me into little pieces to feed to the hogs. I can't. I just. It fills me with dread, Jack, it just fills me with dread. Don't make me go out there. I don't want to go there please, Jack. Don't make me go. Please, Jack. Please. Please don't. Please. Have mercy …

He collapses onto the floor.

JACK: Great!

DELVECCHIO: Sorry, Jack …

JACK: Jesus …

DELVECCHIO: I know.

JACK: What the hell's wrong with you?

DELVECCHIO: I don't know.

JACK: Look: your girlfriend fucked around on you. You've been wounded. But we've talked about this. You've got to get back out there. It's the only way.

DELVECCHIO: Yeah. Drive five hours to stare down the barrel of a gun at some demented crazy woman.

JACK: You're just driving out to the country, Delvecchio. It's not like you're going off to war.

DELVECCHIO: It feels like war.

JACK: Great. This is just great. Christ. OK. Listen to me. Get up off the floor. Get up off the floor and dust yourself --— Dust yourself off. Show a little dignity, eh? For God's sake … *(DELVECCHIO gets up off the floor)* Good. Now. Listen to me. Clearly you're more fucked up than any of us realized, but I don't have the energy to deal with you right now. Go out and do something, anything, OK? I don't care. Go get hosed. Get laid if you're up to it. But whatever you do, Delvecchio, get the hell out of here before anyone else sees you like this. It's not the time to be showing any weakness around here. Now get out of my hair. I've got things to do.

> DELVECCHIO *leaves the stage, muttering under his breath.*

> *Blackout.*

∼

THIRTEEN *JAPANESE AVANT-GARDE CINEMA*

> *Lights up, dim.* JACK *and* AMBER *as if at Broccoli. Images such as those described are projected on them. The scene begins with an Asian avant garde*

musical soundscape, the sound of a projector, and a long silence as they watch the film.

JACK: Holy. Mother. Of God.

Pause.

Five hours ... six lines ... mind-numbing ... .

Pause.

AMBER: This is so cool ...

Pause. JACK looks over at AMBER. She looks at him. He smiles wanly. She smiles demurely.

Soooo very cool ...

Pause.

JACK: It would seem to have something to do with a horse. A pale grey horse. And an old man in an orange jump suit who walks by the sea ... Beyond this I know nothing ...

Pause.

JACK: Mind-numbing ... .

Pause.

AMBER: It's so beautiful. So simple. So elegant. So bleak. It makes you want to go home and burn all your furniture ... or something ...

Pause. JACK looks around, at the other people in the audience.

JACK: At least there can't possibly be anyone I know here. Can there? There'd better not be. Brother. I don't know about this ... I mean, what was Darlene asking me for, anyway? Some attention. Maybe that's all any of us want: someone to pay close attention. Why can't I do that for her? Why am I here? We're supposed to be having a date. Is this how I show that I love her? *(He glances at* AMBER.*)* But who could say no to this? What red-blooded male could say no to this? God help me …

> *Slight pause.*

AMBER: It's great. Just great. But I don't know. Like, nothing's great, like totally great, for five hours. Five hours. God. Maybe we should just cut to the chase and go back to my place. I don't want to fall asleep … I should never have gone to yoga this morning … five hours … but it's so good … soooo interesting … but it's five hours … and it's been such a long day and so long since anyone said anything … .

> *She yawns and closes her eyes. Her head nods over and falls on* JACK*'s shoulder. Her hands spill onto his lap.* JACK *remains stiff as a board, discretely looking around him to see if anyone has noticed.*

JACK: This is great, just great. God. Am I the only one still awake in here? What the hell is this shit?! What on earth are you doing here, you fool? You should just go home. Stop the madness and just go home. Chew off your arm and go home. And you'll laugh about it in the morning—

> AMBER *stirs and looks at him. He smiles back like an idiot. She puts her arms around his neck and kisses him. He kisses her back. She stands and takes him by the hand and together they leave, stopping for one more kiss.*

> JACK *remains, while* AMBER *leaves the stage.*

~

FOURTEEN *THEY HUNG A POET*

> *JACK in a single spotlight. He has a ring of keys in his hand. He checks his watch.*

JACK: Holy cow. Four o'clock. *(He checks again)* Five o'clock! Oh God. This is trouble. Serious trouble. OK. Here's how it was. How was it? OK. There was a situation .... A crisis. Yeah. There was a crisis. In production. That sounds reasonable. A crisis in production. International implications. A corrupt dictatorship. Violations of human rights all over the place. Atrocities. They hung a poet. Same old story. We had to get our men out of there. By the time I realized how late it was, I thought it best not to call. I thought you might be asleep. I was hoping you'd be asleep. I hope you're asleep. God. Just don't wake up. Don't be awake. If there's a god, don't be awake. I'll sleep in Emily's room. I never meant ... . Oh God. What was I thinking?

> *Lights fade to black.*

END OF ACT ONE

ACT TWO

~

FIFTEEN *HUMPIN'*

DELVECCHIO approaches JACK.

DELVECCHIO:	Did you get your hair cut or something?
JACK:	No.
DELVECCHIO:	You been to Moores?
JACK:	What?
DELVECCHIO:	Get a new suit?
JACK:	No. Why?
DELVECCHIO:	I just like your suit, that's all.
JACK:	Thanks.
DELVECCHIO:	It's great. I really like the pleating action on those pants.
JACK:	Oh yeah …
DELVECCHIO:	It's really sharp.
JACK:	Thanks.
DELVECCHIO:	And the vents on your jacket —
JACK:	Delvecchio. Never mind that now. I need to talk to you.
DELVECCHIO:	OK.
JACK:	I've just talked to Kelly.
DELVECCHIO:	Yeah? What kind of mood's he in?
JACK:	Kelly is in an extremely hostile mood.
DELVECCHIO:	Sounds bad.
JACK:	It is bad, Delvecchio. And it's particularly bad for you.
DELVECCHIO:	Oh?
JACK:	Yes.
DELVECCHIO:	Like for me personally?
JACK:	Yes.

DELVECCHIO: On account of the Horton thing?

JACK: That's part of it.

DELVECCHIO: 'Cause I wanted to say that I went out last night, had a few cocktails and just basically chilled and I feel like I'm moving forward, you know? To a place where —

JACK: Do you read your email, Delvecchio?

DELVECCHIO: Yeah …

JACK: You do, do you?

DELVECCHIO: Of course.

JACK: Even the stuff from upstairs?

DELVECCHIO: Especially the stuff from upstairs.

JACK: Did you see the one about the fact that the company had started monitoring your Internet use?

DELVECCHIO: Say what?

JACK: Or did that one get by you?

DELVECCHIO: What do you mean monitor?

JACK: You don't know what it means to monitor something?

DELVECCHIO: They've been monitoring what I've been doing on the Internet?

JACK: Yeah.

DELVECCHIO: Who?

JACK: Guess.

DELVECCHIO: Not Kelly.

JACK: Yeah. Well, Kelly's people.

DELVECCHIO: Like, monitoring all of it?

JACK: Every last word.

DELVECCHIO: Oh.

JACK: Every last dot dot dot … .

Slight pause.

JACK: So …

DELVECCHIO: Yeah …

JACK: You've been a busy boy.

DELVECCHIO: Yeah.

JACK: A very busy boy.

DELVECCHIO: Yeah.

JACK: Humpin'.

DELVECCHIO: Excuse me?

JACK: That's what we used to call it. Humpin'. It's a verb. You've been humpin' women all over the world, eh? All kinds of women, all different ages, and you've been in all sorts of disguises. "Eyes like shattered emeralds in snow ..."

DELVECCHIO: They saw that one?

JACK: They've got that one taped to the fridge door in the coffee room up there.

DELVECCHIO: Serious?

JACK: Dead serious.

DELVECCHIO: Shit.

JACK: Yeah. I'd say that right now, the Horton thing is the least of your worries.

DELVECCHIO: Right.

JACK: You're being paid pretty damned well to sit on your ass, humpin' all day.

DELVECCHIO: Yeah.

JACK: So what do you think I should say to Kelly about this, hmmm? Like, in your defence. What would you say to Kelly, if you were me?

DELVECCHIO: I don't know.

JACK: I don't either. Any suggestion you could make would be greatly appreciated. This is my floor. It was one thing to sit on my hands and watch Sawchuck go down. But there's a difference. Sawchuck wasn't pulling his weight. You have been. At least, up until a few weeks ago. Until you finally figured out what the rest of us knew anyway about that gal of yours.

DELVECCHIO: Yeah ...

JACK:	Because I'm in an extremely generous mood today, I'm going to help you through this. OK?
DELVECCHIO:	OK.
JACK:	OK. So. Where are you, Delvecchio? Hmmm? Where the hell are you?
DELVECCHIO:	I don't know.
JACK:	Well, you're sitting in the tall grass, that's for sure. You've got yourself a bit of a bad lie right now? Eh?
DELVECCHIO:	Yeah.
JACK:	Trees in front of you. Sand traps all around. Water you can't even see but it's out there. You're sitting in the weeds. So what are you going to do? Hmmm? Pack up your clubs and slink off the course? Drive home like a wimp? I don't think so. You've got a shot to play, and you're going to play it. You see, when you get to be my age, Delvecchio, you live for shots like this. For the challenge of it. The opportunity. These perfect little moments we find in our lives, when we can step up and nail that sucker. And what a feeling, eh? When you play that horrible, shitty shot you've left yourself and you nail it. You watch the ball loft up in the air like that, that perfect approach coming out of the rough. It can be so beautiful. Like you think maybe your ball will never come down, that it'll just hang there in that blue sky suspended over the flag stick, beautiful, that little white ball framed like that. Beautiful …
DELVECCHIO:	You OK there, Jack?
JACK:	I'm great. I am great. We're going to make that shot, Delvecchio. Right?
DELVECCHIO:	Right.
JACK:	So what do we do? What do we say? Hmmm? What do we say?
DELVECCHIO:	I look at it this way. I had more or less a breakdown. I lost it. I obviously went to the bad place. But I couldn't help it. And you know, I've given this some thought, and I can't help but feel a little hard done by. Some places

would have put me on some kind of short-term disability. Some kind of compassionate leave. But I come back and all anyone gives a shit about is the Horton thing. You could have helped. Kelly could have helped. Someone could have jumped in their car and driven out there. Taken some of the pressure off of me. But all anyone seems to care about is ragging me about it.

JACK: Well, unfortunately, Delvecchio, no one gives a shit about all that. This is an oil company. If I walk upstairs and say you've lost your hard-on for that contract, then you're done. Finished. And not just here but anywhere else because word gets around. Anyway, the whole world's under a lot of stress. That's not going to help much. What else?

DELVECCHIO: I don't know. We could say that it's common?

JACK: Common?

DELVECCHIO: Yeah.

JACK: That's our defence? That it's common.

DELVECCHIO: Yeah.

JACK: Tell me something. I don't know these things. Is it common?

DELVECCHIO: Oh yeah.

JACK: Amazing …

DELVECCHIO: In fact, I'd go so far as to say it's rampant.

JACK: Is it really?

DELVECCHIO: Oh yeah. Everyone's doing it. Everywhere. You walk through a bank, it looks like everyone's working, looking after your money or whatever, except they're not. Either they're playing solitaire, or they're sitting in chat rooms trying to get lucky.

JACK: You're saying when I walk into my bank and everyone's looking at their computers, what they're actually doing is humpin'?

DELVECCHIO: Oh yeah. I've chatted with people in banks.

JACK: Really?

DELVECCHIO: Oh yeah. Lots of times.

JACK: Not the Royal Bank ... .

DELVECCHIO: I'm not sure.

JACK: Where else?

DELVECCHIO: Government offices, doctors offices, funeral homes, schools. You name it.

JACK: You're saying you've humped someone in a funeral home?

DELVECCHIO: Oh yeah.

JACK: Holy Mother of God. And you just, what? Do it? But with words? You type in the words or something? Is that how it works?

DELVECCHIO: Something like that.

JACK: You type something in, and this turns someone on?

DELVECCHIO: Yes.

JACK: It excites them?

DELVECCHIO: That's the general idea.

JACK: Unbelievable. Well, on any account, the fact that it's common —

DELVECCHIO: Rampant —

JACK: Whatever. It's not going to appease Kelly a whole lot. He's very interested in making you a whipping boy on this thing. I've got to figure out a strategy for dealing with him. Maybe I'm an old fashioned guy, I don't know. But I actually care for the people who work for me. I actually care for you. Like, we've golfed together, right? I don't golf with people I don't care for.

DELVECCHIO: I always liked golfing with you, Jack ...

JACK: I've always like golfing with you too, Del. And there's something I've got to tell you.

DELVECCHIO: Yes?

JACK: I think your short game is probably as good as I've seen.

DELVECCHIO: No.

JACK: No. I do.

DELVECCHIO: Thanks, Jack. That means a lot.

JACK: I mean it.

DELVECCHIO: Thank you.

JACK: Listen. Lay a bit low for a couple of days. OK? Stay out of sight. Don't go upstairs, whatever you do. Kelly's really got his nuts in a knot right now. He's the last person you want to run into right now. OK?

DELVECCHIO: OK.

JACK: OK.

～

SIXTEEN *THRONE OF BLOOD*

AMBER *approaches* DELVECCHIO.

AMBER: Hi, Delvecchio.

DELVECCHIO: Hi, Amber. How's it going?

AMBER: Good. Great. Fantastic, actually. I can't believe this place.

DELVECCHIO: Oh yeah?

AMBER: Yeah. Like, I get this memo from someone upstairs. Giving me the green light on a video. Only they want it right away. Like, yesterday. Can you believe that?

DELVECCHIO: That's great. Congratulations.

AMBER: Thanks. I can't believe it. Everything's happening so fast.

DELVECCHIO: Yeah, well that's the nature of the business.

AMBER: Right. So, how are you doing?

DELVECCHIO: OK, I guess.

AMBER: Yeah?

DELVECCHIO: Yeah.

AMBER: Just OK?

DELVECCHIO: Just working through some stuff. No biggie.

AMBER: Right.

Slight pause.

DELVECCHIO: Hey!

AMBER: What?

DELVECCHIO: Guess what.

AMBER: What?

DELVECCHIO: I went out and rented a great movie the other night.

AMBER: Oh?

DELVECCHIO: Film.

AMBER: Yeah?

DELVECCHIO: Yeah. I rented a great film the other night.

AMBER: You?

DELVECCHIO: Yeah.

AMBER: What was it?

AMBER: *Throne of Blood.* Ever heard of it?

AMBER: *Throne of Blood?* Are you kidding?!

DELVECCHIO: No.

AMBER: You saw *Throne of Blood?*

DELVECCHIO: Yepper. By what'shisname.

AMBER: Akira Kurosawa.

DELVECCHIO: Right. Japanese, eh?

AMBER: I know. So, what did you think?

DELVECCHIO: I loved it.

AMBER: Really?

DELVECCHIO: Oh yeah. You like him?

AMBER: He's a master. What's not to like?

DELVECCHIO: Exactly. I loved the violence.

AMBER: Oh yeah?

DELVECCHIO: Yeah.

AMBER:	Me too.
DELVECCHIO:	I mean, don't get me wrong. I'm not a violent person.
AMBER:	Me neither.
DELVECCHIO:	But I like watching it.
AMBER:	Me too.
DELVECCHIO:	Serious?
AMBER:	Oh yeah. Totally.
DELVECCHIO:	Cool.
AMBER:	It's just so visceral.
DELVECCHIO:	Isn't it just?
AMBER:	Absolutely.
DELVECCHIO:	Just so bloody visceral.
AMBER:	Actually, in the same way, there's also some pornography I like to watch.
DELVECCHIO:	Are you shitting me?
AMBER:	No.
DELVECCHIO:	You have to be shitting me.
AMBER:	I'm not. I like watching, you know, I guess, things I've never done myself. But maybe I've wanted to do them, but haven't known I've wanted to do them until I've seen someone else doing them. You know?
DELVECCHIO:	Listen. Are you going to go out with me, or what?
AMBER:	Unfortunately, right now, I can't.
DELVECCHIO:	You can't?
AMBER:	I shouldn't.
DELVECCHIO:	Why not?
AMBER:	I'm seeing someone.
DELVECCHIO:	You are?
AMBER:	Yes.
DELVECCHIO:	Since we talked last?
AMBER:	Yes.
DELVECCHIO:	Bummer …

AMBER: I'm sorry.

DELVECCHIO: That's a drag …

AMBER: Although …

DELVECCHIO: What?

AMBER: It doesn't mean that we couldn't grab a coffee sometime and talk some more. About Kurosawa. Or current trends in Japanese cinema. Or whatever.

DELVECCHIO: That'd be OK?

AMBER: Yeah. I mean. I'm seeing someone. But it's not like I'm planning on getting married to him or anything like that.

DELVECCHIO: Cool.

AMBER: Yeah.

DELVECCHIO: Maybe we could pick up where we left off.

AMBER: Sure.

DELVECCHIO: OK. Well. Shit. I've got to get back. I'll guess I'll come and grab you then. Sometime.

AMBER: Yeah. You do that.

DELVECCHIO: Yeah. OK. For now, I'm in kinda major shit, so I better blast.

AMBER: OK. I'll see ya.

DELVECCHIO: Yeah. See ya.

~

SEVENTEEN   *CONTROL*

JACK: The situation at home: grim, grim, grim.

DELVECCHIO: Good good good.

JACK: Grim grim grim.

DELVECCHIO: This is good.

JACK: This is bad.

DELVECCHIO: This is about as good as it gets.

JACK:	Of course Darlene suspects the worst.
DELVECCHIO:	Signed, sealed and delivered.
JACK:	She's carrying on like an Old Testament prophet — fire and brimstone and the threat of eternal damnation.
DELVECCHIO:	The babe of the century is going to grab a coffee with me.
JACK:	It just gets more and more depressing every day, a living nightmare.
DELVECCHIO:	A dream come true.
AMBER:	God. Focus, Amber. I mean, OK, there's a lot of men around here. So what? Never mind them. Focus. This could be your big break … .
JACK:	Not that we talk about it, exactly, but she knows something's up and now she spends every last ounce of her energy tormenting me. I suppose, this is what comes of doing bad things.
DELVECCHIO:	The only bad thing about it, is that it's just a coffee.
JACK:	Especially bad things that actually bring you pleasure.
DELVECCHIO:	I mean it's great.
JACK:	The gods find out about it and they fuck you over, big time.
DELVECCHIO:	But what does coffee ever lead to?
JACK:	They cut off your foot or chain you to a cliff or something. Leave you to wallow in your guilt …
DELVECCHIO:	If only I could get her to throw some booze down her throat … .
JACK:	And if the gods don't find out about it, then your wife does, which is probably worse.
DELVECCHIO:	Then anything might be possible.
JACK:	And yet, I don't know … .
AMBER:	The trouble is, you get drawn in, whether you want to or not, you get drawn into people's lives, whether it's right or wrong, it just happens, it doesn't matter where you are, at school, at work, it happens, it just happens …

JACK:	I don't know, really, if I even care.
DELVECCHIO:	And then there's the hammer.
JACK:	I know I should care, but I don't know if I do care. Really.
DELVECCHIO:	She watches pornography.
JACK:	Last night I actually slept, instead of lying there listening to my body fall apart.
DELVECCHIO:	Watches it, studies it, learns from it.
JACK:	My body is trying to teach me something, and I will learn from it. If it kills me.
DELVECCHIO:	And not just stuff from the corner store. This is high brow university pornography we're talking about.
JACK:	So let the gods do to me what they will. I can't change anything now.
DELVECCHIO:	How much better can it get than that?
AMBER:	And the next thing you know, you find yourself thinking about them, too much, and before you know it you're a month behind in your work and I don't know what it is about this place, but it's very hard to stay on course, somehow, very difficult not to get swept away somehow...

EIGHTEEN *BALLS*

JACK and AMBER, who is holding an ornate oriental box.

AMBER:	Hi.
JACK:	Hi.
AMBER:	How are you?
JACK:	Good, good. (Looking wildly around.) Good. Good. Good. How are you?
AMBER:	Good.

JACK:	Good.
AMBER:	So, it's all good?
JACK:	It's all good. Yes. It's all good.
AMBER:	It is?
JACK:	Absolutely.
AMBER:	You sure?
JACK:	Oh sure. All good.
AMBER:	Yeah?
JACK:	Yeah. It's good.

Slight pause.

AMBER:	Too bad about the film.
JACK:	Yeah …
AMBER:	I'm sorry you found it boring.
JACK:	Yeah. Well, I at least managed to stay awake.
AMBER:	Right.
JACK:	Not like some people.
AMBER:	Well, I woke up later. Eventually.
JACK:	You certainly did. Actually, you know, now that I've had a bit of time to, you know, reflect on the film, I think it was actually probably quite interesting. More interesting than it seemed at the time.
AMBER:	Really?
JACK:	Yeah. Like the thing about the horse was very deep, I thought.
AMBER:	Yeah.
JACK:	Like, the symbolism, you know, of the horse, was quite symbolic, I thought.
AMBER:	Symbolic?
JACK:	Especially when they set it on fire. I hope that was done with trick photography.
AMBER:	It wasn't.
JACK:	No?!

AMBER:	That's why it was so intense.
JACK:	No guff … .
AMBER:	So …
JACK:	Yeah …
AMBER:	So, I wasn't sure about this … .
JACK:	Oh?
AMBER:	Yeah.
JACK:	About what, exactly?
AMBER:	You know. Seeing each other. Whatever.
JACK:	It's OK. Honey.
AMBER:	Really?
JACK:	Yeah.
AMBER:	You're sure?
JACK:	Yeah. Everything's OK.
AMBER:	And you're OK?
JACK:	Yeah. I'm OK.
AMBER:	What about at home?
JACK:	Oh. Well, that's kinda, more or less, you know … .
AMBER:	No, I don't know.
JACK:	Don't worry about it. That's my affair.
AMBER:	Oh yeah?
JACK:	Yeah. Don't worry about it.
AMBER:	Right. Well. Anyway. I have something for you.
JACK:	*(Looking around)* You do?
AMBER:	Am I keeping you?
JACK:	No. No. Of course not. I just have a meeting with Lindsay. You know. Upstairs. Whenever.
AMBER:	You mean like, the Lindsay? Like the CEO?
JACK:	Yeah. We have a few things to bat around.
AMBER:	You better go then.
JACK:	No no. It's OK.
AMBER:	Are you sure?

JACK: Yeah. We're friends. We golf.

AMBER: OK. Well, anyway, I was thinking about you, I guess. I didn't know whether I should be or not, but I was. And it doesn't have to mean anything, or anything, but I got you a little present. Here.

> *She hands him a small ornate oriental box.*

AMBER: Go ahead. Open it.

JACK: Right.

> *He opens the box. The box is lined with a bright fabric, and contains two Chinese iron balls.*

Wow … .

AMBER: You like them?

JACK: Yeah … what are they?

AMBER: They're Chinese iron balls. Like, from China? Haven't you seen them?

JACK: I don't think I have.

AMBER: *(Taking one of them from the box)* You roll them in the palm of your hand like so, and they make music. If you're doing it right.

> *She rolls the ball in the palm of her hand and it makes music.*

JACK: Oh yeah.

AMBER: Cool eh?

JACK: Yes. It is.

AMBER: They're supposed to help you relax. Try it.

JACK: OK.

> *He takes the other ball and rolls it in his hand. It makes music.*

AMBER: There you go …

JACK: Hey. That's kinda neat.

AMBER: Yeah.

They stand there rolling the balls in their hands.

The other night. After the film. When you came over. I
had a great time. I wanted you to know. Maybe it's
because I've just been with younger guys before. Like, my
age. They're always in a big hurry to get through things.
But I really liked the way you took your time, the way
you lingered, I guess you'd say. It was amazing, actually.
So I wanted to give you something. That's all.

JACK: Thanks … It was. You know. That thing with the. Wow. It
was just kinda one of those things … .

*Slight pause. She gives him back the ball she's been
rolling.*

AMBER: I should let you get up to see Mr. Lindsay.

JACK: Right. I guess I probably should. Thanks for the present.

AMBER: You're welcome.

JACK: You really are a very thoughtful young woman. Very
refreshing.

AMBER: Thanks … Hey. Listen.

JACK: Yes?

AMBER: You know … these balls …

JACK: Yes?

AMBER: I don't know if I should — But. You see, I've heard of
other things you can do with them …

JACK: Oh?

AMBER: Yeah. Just if you're interested.

JACK: Like what?

AMBER: I probably shouldn't say here.

JACK: No?

AMBER: I don't know.

JACK: Go ahead.

AMBER: Well, like intimate things, I guess you'd say.

JACK:	Oh?
AMBER:	Yeah. Quite exotic. A friend of mine showed me.
JACK:	Oh?!
AMBER:	Yeah.
JACK:	That certainly sounds intriguing.
AMBER:	I was thinking. If you wanted to. Like I know you're busy. But if you wanted to. Sometime. I could show you.
JACK:	Sure.
AMBER:	Yeah?
JACK:	Oh yeah.
AMBER:	You're not too busy?
JACK:	I can always get away.
AMBER:	Do you want to come over?
JACK:	Yes.
AMBER:	Cool. Like tonight?
JACK:	Absolutely.
AMBER:	Cool. So I'll see you later. Around nine? Is that good?
JACK:	Nine.
AMBER:	Is that OK?
JACK:	Hmmm. That could be a bit of a problem. Could we make it a bit earlier?
AMBER:	OK. When?
JACK:	Let's see. Maybe around 6:30 or so?
AMBER:	6:30?!
JACK:	It's just that I kinda have something on around nine with my. You know.
AMBER:	I see.
JACK:	Is that OK? Around 6:30?
AMBER:	I guess. I mean, don't worry about it if you're too busy.
JACK:	I'm not too busy. I just have this thing. That's all. And I'd really like to see you again. Because. It was, like you were saying, like — Absolutely. It's just sometimes, you know. Hey. Come here.

He hugs her.

AMBER: I just worry about this, you know?

JACK: There's nothing to worry about.

AMBER: No?

JACK: No. Absolutely nothing for us to worry about. It's all good.

> *He kisses her. At this moment,* DELVECCHIO *approaches them. He stops and watches the kiss. They don't see him.* DELVECCHIO *withdraws.*

JACK: So, I'll see you tonight.

AMBER: Right.

JACK: I'll be sure to bring my balls.

~

NINETEEN   *THE CYCLICAL NATURE OF LOVE*

> JACK *with a high iron.*

JACK: So then Darlene says, they have counsellors. As if I didn't know that. People you can talk to. Yeah, I know what counsellors are. The thing is, I don't want to talk to anyone. She asks why. I say, it's none of their damned business. She says, it's our business. They make it theirs. That's what they do. They're professionals. And I say, some things need time. That's all. I say, Leave it. She says we can't just leave it. So I set her down in a chair so I can explain how it is. I say listen. There's peaks. And there's valleys. You know? Peaks. And valleys. OK. I'll admit, we're in a bit of a valley right now. It's true. But that's only natural. It's all part of the cyclical nature of love. You know? The peaks and valleys. And the cyclical nature of love. But we'll come out of it. No one lingers in the valley forever. If only we just leave it. Just leave it in the shadow of the valley. You throw a whole lot of light on it right now, and it'll only spread. It'll only grow and fester. Like a cancer. In the revealing light, it'll just grow and grow and grow until it's out of control. But left in the shadowy darkness, eventually it will shrivel up and die. And then we move on. To the next peak. And she says, is that what you really believe? Leave it in the dark? And I said, yes, I do. Away from the light. And she looks at me and says you're wrong. She says I'm wrong. She says I don't know anything about human relationships. Or even being human for that matter. And so I say, as long as I'm calling the shots around here, you won't be dragging me off to a counsellor like some kind of whipped school boy. We leave it alone. And everything will be just fine. And she heard me. She said OK. And I said OK. And so, it would seem, it's OK. Everything's OK.

~

TWENTY *SHOCKED AND APPALLED*

DELVECCHIO: I went up and saw Kelly.

JACK: You what?! Why did you do that? What possible reason could you have to go up and see Kelly?

DELVECCHIO: I thought it was something I needed to do. To clear the air.

JACK: Shit. What kind of mood was he in?

DELVECCHIO: OK.

JACK: OK?!

DELVECCHIO: Yeah.

JACK: What did you talk about?

DELVECCHIO: Usual bullshit.

JACK: You and Kelly don't have usual bullshit. What were you talking about?

DELVECCHIO: This that. The other thing.

JACK: What other thing?!

DELVECCHIO: The Horton thing. What else would I talk to Kelly about?

JACK: You tell me.

DELVECCHIO: Like I said, usual bullshit.

JACK: You see, I don't even know why you'd be talking to him about the Horton thing.

DELVECCHIO: You said he was out to get me.

JACK: Yes.

DELVECCHIO: Because of the Horton thing.

JACK: Yes.

DELVECCHIO: And the Internet thing.

JACK: Yes —

DELVECCHIO: So I told him my side of the story.

JACK: But you told your side of the story. To me.

DELVECCHIO: Yeah?

JACK: So you didn't have to tell Kelly yourself.

DELVECCHIO: You don't think so.

JACK: No.

DELVECCHIO: Why?

JACK: Because I already told him. That's my job. To tell Kelly what's going on.

DELVECCHIO: Well, he didn't seem to have any clear idea of what was going on.

JACK: That's not my fault.

DELVECCHIO: Then whose fault is it?

JACK: I don't know. But it's not mine. I told him. I can't help it if he doesn't listen.

DELVECCHIO: It doesn't matter, Jack. He knows now.

JACK: It does matter.

DELVECCHIO: No it doesn't.

JACK: Yes it does. It matters to me. Because it's my job. That's part of my job. To manage things. The stuff down here. The stuff that comes down from up there. I manage this department. That's what I do. I'm a manager. I manage the people under me. If every time something happens, the people from this floor just walk upstairs into Kelly's office and sit down and put their feet up on his desk and have a good old yak, then it looks like I'm not doing my job. Now Kelly's going to be all over my ass. You see? Because of what you did.

DELVECCHIO: Kelly's not going to be all over your ass.

JACK: You think not?

DELVECCHIO: He's your brother-in-law.

JACK: You don't know him like I do. He's a shark. He's got fucking ice water in his veins. He's going to. Jesus. I can't believe. I just can't. Fuck! Why the fuck?! Christ …

Slight pause. JACK breathes.

DELVECCHIO: I've got to tell you, Jack … .

JACK: What?

DELVECCHIO: Today, earlier, I saw you and Amber by the elevator.

JACK: Yeah?

DELVECCHIO: Well …

JACK: Well what?

DELVECCHIO: I've got to tell you, I was shocked. Shocked and appalled by what I saw.

JACK: What the hell are you talking about?

DELVECCHIO: You and Amber. By the elevator.

JACK: Oh, brother. You saw — ? Christ. That was nothing, Delvecchio. OK?

DELVECCHIO: Oh, it sure looked like something to me.

JACK: It was nothing. You saw nothing.

DELVECCHIO: You call that nothing?

JACK: That's exactly what I call it.

DELVECCHIO: Well, it sure looked like something to me —

JACK: It looked like nothing. Because it is nothing. OK? Nothing. You saw nothing. Because there is nothing. It is nothing. There is nothing to ask. Nothing to see. Nothing.

Slight pause.

DELVECCHIO: How's Darlene doing these days?

JACK: Fuck off.

DELVECCHIO: She's a good lady, Jack. She doesn't deserve it.

JACK: It's none of your business.

DELVECCHIO: It is actually. You know? After the last time, and everything I went through, I thought I could trust you of all people to keep your hands off of Amber.

JACK: Who are you to talk? Sitting in your office, humpin' strangers all day.

DELVECCHIO: That's different.

JACK: Bullshit.

DELVECCHIO: It is.

JACK: How is it different?

DELVECCHIO: It's not real. It's just words.

JACK: But they're written by someone.

DELVECCHIO: Not someone you'll ever meet.

JACK: There's still a person behind them.

DELVECCHIO: No one gets touched.

JACK: So?

DELVECCHIO: So no one gets hurt.

JACK: So that makes it OK?

DELVECCHIO: Basically, yeah.

JACK: So the crime these days is to actually touch someone? To actually touch another human being? Is that it?

DELVECCHIO: In some cases.

JACK: But it's OK to sit alone in your room and hump someone you don't even know? In some other corner of the world? As long as there's no human contact? Is that what you think?

DELVECCHIO: If the human being you're talking about is young enough to be your daughter, and if you're already married to someone else, then I think, yeah. You're better off alone in your room.

JACK: If that's what you think, then I think you're fucked.

DELVECCHIO: It's not just me. That's how everyone thinks.

JACK: Then everyone's fucked.

DELVECCHIO: It's how everyone in the world thinks, Jack. No fuss, no muss. No one gets hurt. If you weren't so out of touch, you'd be able to figure that out for yourself.

JACK: Get out of here.

DELVECCHIO: Fine!

JACK: And if you breathe a word of this to anyone, you'll be digging up weeds with Sawchuck, you understand?!

~

TWENTY-ONE   *SECOND CUP*

AMBER and DELVECCHIO at a café, each with a Styrofoam cup.

DELVECCHIO: Well, this is a nice surprise.

AMBER: What?

DELVECCHIO: Us being together here, like this.

AMBER: Yeah, it is.

DELVECCHIO: 'Cause, you know, you said you were with this other guy and stuff. And so I thought like, maybe I was just getting in the way, or whatever.

AMBER: I never thought that. Anyway, it's just a coffee, right?

DELVECCHIO: Yeah, I guess. Just a coffee …

Slight pause.

DELVECCHIO: How is your mochacino?

AMBER: Good. How's your Americano?

DELVECCHIO: Great … You want a Bailey's or something with that?

AMBER: No thanks.

DELVECCHIO: Grand Marnier?

AMBER: That's OK.

DELVECCHIO: Jaegermeister?

AMBER: I'm not really into drinking all that much.

DELVECCHIO: No?

AMBER: Not really. Are you?

DELVECCHIO: No. Not really. Well. Maybe a little bit. Socially, you know. Because, let's face it, all roads lead to the bar it seems. In this business, anyway … .

AMBER: Right …

Pause.

AMBER: So, you really liked *Throne of Blood?*

DELVECCHIO: Yeah. It's amazing. I'm glad I watched it.

AMBER: I'm glad you watched it, too. You surprised me.

DELVECCHIO: Yeah, well I'm full of surprises.

AMBER: I'm sure you are.

DELVECCHIO: I'd like to see more of his stuff.

AMBER: It's all good.

DELVECCHIO: Does he have anything new coming out?

AMBER: No. He's dead.

DELVECCHIO: Right … Makes it kind of hard, eh … ?

AMBER: Yeah …

Slight pause.

DELVECCHIO: Sometimes I wish I'd lived back then. In a different time. And place. Where you could, you know, say someone did something to you, something bad, it would have to be bad, really bad, and you could just take your sword down off the wall and get yourself some retribution. You know?

AMBER: Kinda …

DELVECCHIO: You could do a film about that. Like modern day. A guy gets pissed off, takes his big sword down off the wall and Look out.

AMBER: Right …

DELVECCHIO: I mean, it's been done with guns. Done to death. But I just think there'd be something therapeutic about being able to hack some back-stabbing bastard with a big sword.

AMBER: I guess …

DELVECCHIO: Yeah. A great big sharp honking sword … .

Slight pause.

AMBER: So, the other day in the coffee room?

DELVECCHIO: Yeah?

AMBER: You were talking about your girlfriend? Screwing around on you?

DELVECCHIO: Yeah?

AMBER: Is that how you feel about it?

DELVECCHIO: What?

AMBER: Like you want revenge or something? Blood? Like you want to hack someone?

DELVECCHIO: Oh, I don't know. Not really. I don't know. Well. Maybe. Maybe a little bit. It may have crossed my mind. Yeah. Maybe. In a couple of cases. Sure. Probably. Yeah. Absolutely. Bring it on! What the hell?

AMBER: Like, her? Or the guys? Or what?

DELVECCHIO: I don't know. You know? The guys. They're all in the bar and they buy you a beer and slap you on the back and they think you don't know anything. They just think you're a clown. And yet you have to work with them. Some of them you have to work with every day. Some of

them you have to work for, you have to answer to them.
So what can you do? I guess you dream of running them
through or something. You know?

AMBER: Yeah.

DELVECCHIO: But they're not really worth it. They're not really worth
the effort. They'll get theirs. Oh yeah. They'll get theirs,
alright. And as for Sharon, that was her name, that's
different, I guess. That can be quite hard on your self-
esteem, when you sense that there's something going on
but you don't know for sure and you start thinking you're
going crazy. You think you're imagining things but you
know in your heart that you're not. Like you're home and
you have this feeling that something's wrong, so you try
to keep yourself busy. Tidying. Doing the laundry. She's
gone out. Hasn't said where. You don't know who she's
with. And you don't really want to think about it. But you
can't help it. It keeps running around again and again in
your mind. You end up doing a lot of laundry 'cause it
makes you feel like you're in control. Because you can
fold a shirt. You can touch something of hers. But there's
only so much laundry you can do ….

She reaches across the table and holds his hand.

DELVECCHIO: Thing is, once the trust is gone, it's gone. You know? I
don't know. I think. That's the bottom line. Trust. Maybe
revenge would help. Violence of some kind. I don't know.
When you get right down to it, none of them are even
worth it. I just thought it was a good idea for a movie.
Film.

AMBER: No. That's probably a movie you're talking about.

DELVECCHIO: Right

Slight pause.

AMBER: I'm kinda surprised you'd tell me all that.

DELVECCHIO: Oh? Sorry.

AMBER: Don't be sorry. That's not what I meant. It's just that most people you meet don't really bother to tell you what they're feeling, exactly. You know?

DELVECCHIO: I guess.

AMBER: You're always guessing.

DELVECCHIO: Yeah.

AMBER: Always reading between the lines. Looking for signs. Looking for clues. Like, they say they're "kinda this" and "kinda that." But they never tell you how they are, or even what they are, exactly. You're supposed to read their minds. And so you never know where you stand. You know?

DELVECCHIO: Right.

AMBER: Like, I know what you're saying about trust. But I think there's also something to be said for honesty.

DELVECCHIO: I suppose.

AMBER: Like, there should be honesty, don't you think?

DELVECCHIO: Yeah. But this would be my question.

AMBER: What?

DELVECCHIO: When does it start? The honesty.

AMBER: I don't know —

DELVECCHIO: For you to be honest, say with me — well first you have to start being honest with yourself. Are you being honest with yourself? Are you being true to yourself? Are you being true to the things you believe? Because if you're not, then there's not much hope for your relationship with me. Or whoever. I just say "me" because I happen to be sitting here having a coffee with you. You know?

AMBER: Yeah.

DELVECCHIO: Yeah?

AMBER: Yeah. I think I know what you're talking about …

DELVECCHIO: Yeah …

Long pause.

AMBER: So … what is Jaegermeister, exactly?

DELVECCHIO: Like bitters or something. I think.

AMBER: Like, booze?

DELVECCHIO: Yeah. Definitely booze. Why? You want one?

AMBER: Yeah. Maybe I will. Would you have one?

DELVECCHIO: Oh yeah! I mean, sure. You sure you want one?

AMBER: Yeah. You have time?

DELVECCHIO: Yeah, I've got time. You got time?

AMBER: I've got time.

DELVECCHIO: Cool.

AMBER: Yeah.

DELVECCHIO: OK. Let's have a Jaegermeister.

~

TWENTY-TWO   *SOMETIMES YOU NEED THE ARMY*

> *JACK, sitting with a bright red cardboard filing box on his knees.* DELVECCHIO *approaches him.*

DELVECCHIO: Isn't it funny? We knew Kelly was gunning for someone. You thought it was me. Turned out to be you. How can you know these things?

JACK: I don't know …

> *Long pause.*

JACK: So, they gave you a raise? Is that what I heard? A raise?

DELVECCHIO: Yeah.

JACK: Why would they give you a raise?

DELVECCHIO: 'Cause of the way we handled the Horton thing.

JACK: We?

DELVECCHIO: Me and Kelly.

JACK: Kelly helped you handle the Horton thing?

DELVECCHIO: Yeah. It was wild. He used to be in the army, eh? Like a Major or some damned thing? Did you know that? I never knew that. So we went in with the army. The actual fucking army. Can you believe that? Those yokels never stood a chance. Kelly couldn't believe you wanted to send me in there by myself.

JACK: I didn't. I told you to call the RCMP.

DELVECCHIO: Well that's the thing about it, eh? Sometimes the RCMP isn't enough. Sometimes you need the army. Anyway, you can't argue with results.

JACK: What about the chat room stuff?

DELVECCHIO: What about it?

JACK: Didn't Kelly have anything to say about that?

DELVECCHIO: He's been to a few himself.

JACK: Kelly?

DELVECCHIO: Oh yeah. Most people have, Jack. Kelly said he just did it on an experimental basis.

JACK: What? He didn't inhale?

DELVECCHIO: I don't know. He figured it was probably good therapy for me. After my relationship went down and everything. What with her going behind my back and destroying my self-esteem and all.

JACK: Therapy …

DELVECCHIO: You know, for all the stuff you've been saying about him over the years, he's actually a pretty decent guy.

JACK: You think Kelly's a decent guy?

DELVECCHIO: Yeah.

JACK: Well I don't.

DELVECCHIO: Maybe you resent him. You know? That happens.

JACK: I have no reason to resent Kelly.

DELVECCHIO: Did you ever stop and ask yourself if maybe it was the age thing?

JACK: What are you talking about?

DELVECCHIO: Maybe you resented Kelly because he's younger than you, yet you had to report to him. And on top of that, being your wife's brother. That's a double whammy. I can see you resenting that.

JACK: I've got an hour to grab my things. That's all. I don't want to waste any more of it with you.

DELVECCHIO: OK, I'm gone. *(He starts to go then stops)* By the way. If you haven't heard it by now, you might as well hear it from me first.

JACK: What?

DELVECCHIO: Kelly was extremely distressed to hear about you and Amber. About you going behind Darlene's back and all. Of course he would be. She's his sister, after all. Yeah. You should have seen the look on his face. The disappointment. The betrayal. Finally, the outrage. And I couldn't help but share his outrage. And I could have told you, 'cause I lived through it. Nothing good ever comes of it. And so I thought it was my duty — my moral and corporate duty — to report what I saw. Anyway. Later, dude.

DELVECCHIO leaves the stage.

~

TWENTY-THREE   *INTO THE LIGHT*

JACK alone.

JACK: Thing he didn't know was that she already knew so it was only a matter of time. She has this friend Margaret. Margaret, who I've met, apparently, but for the life of me I can't remember her, what she looks like. Margaret, who's taking a class in avant-garde cinema at the University. Margaret Ishikawa. Who knew? Who knew she'd be sitting right behind me the whole wretched time? So she asks, Who is it? I say, It doesn't matter. I say, I'm sorry. But it's too late. Because the little creep has brought it into the light. That's the thing, about a well-mannered woman like Darlene: she understands that a situation like this is best left behind closed doors. In the dark. What happens at home, stays at home. But once the little creep brought it into the light, what could she do? She has her pride. And I can't blame her.

Long pause.

JACK: So, I've made arrangements for a sharp little place downtown. It's great. Very clean, very modern. Nice shag carpet. A dishwasher, though I don't plan on eating there much. I like eating out these days. There's some great restaurants in town … not like it used to be. But I've got a lot to do before I move into my new place. Man, sometimes I feel there's hardly enough hours in a day.

JACK sings Fly Me to the Moon *under his breath.*

Continuous to next scene.

TWENTY-FOUR   *FLY ME TO THE MOON …*

JACK and AMBER, at her mother's place.

JACK: *(Singing)* Fly me to the moon, and let me play among the stars. Ba, ba ba ba boo, Ba ba ba boo, ba ba ba ba —

AMBER hands JACK an empty glass.

AMBER: There you go.

JACK: Thanks.

AMBER: You're singing.

JACK: Yeah. Ol' blue eyes …

AMBER: Who?

JACK: Frank Sinatra.

AMBER: Right.

JACK: Yeah. Tonight, I've got a song in my heart. And a flask in my pocket.

           He pulls a flask from his pocket and pours a shot into the glass.

           You want one?

AMBER: I'm fine thanks. I have my tea.

JACK: Right. Tea has its place, I guess. But sometimes a guy needs a good belt of the hard stuff.

AMBER: Right.

JACK: Cheers.

AMBER: Cheers.

JACK: Guess what else.

AMBER: What?

JACK: Guess what else I have in my pocket.

AMBER: Oh. I, I can't.

JACK: *(Pulling out two airplane tickets)* Freedom.

AMBER: I beg your pardon?

JACK: Freedom. Singapore Airlines, honey. You ever flown them?

AMBER: No …

JACK: Beautiful airline. It makes you realize how bad the situation is in this country when you fly with these guys. They give you the little slippers. You know? The slippers. And the mask. The eye mask. And this special nasal gel you rub inside your nostrils. Beautiful stuff.

AMBER: I don't understand …

JACK: Well, it's pretty simple. I've got two tickets to Singapore. A week from today. That gives us a bit of time to get our affairs in order. And before you know it, we'll be sitting at the Long Bar at Raffles Hotel, sipping on a Singapore Sling. That's where they invented it. And after that, well, the sky's the limit. We can hop around, up to Jakarta, down to Oz, over to Tokyo to catch a film. Together, we can explore the mysteries of the Orient ...

AMBER: Just you and me?

JACK: Just you and me.

AMBER: I see.

JACK: Pretty cool, eh?

AMBER: Oh yeah ...

JACK: So what do you think?

AMBER: Well, uh. Jeez. Where to begin ... . ?

JACK: Is something wrong?

AMBER: Yeah, kinda, I guess.

JACK: Is it the Singapore thing?

AMBER: No, it's not that ...

JACK: Because nothing's written in stone, we could go anywhere. These are full fare tickets. I could change them. Paris. Cuba. Wherever.

AMBER: No, no, Jack. Listen: it's not where. It's the whole — you know?

JACK: What?

AMBER: It's the whole idea of a trip right now.

JACK: Yeah?

AMBER: I can't just take off and leave.

JACK: Why not?

AMBER: My job, for one thing. I just started. I can't just up and leave.

JACK: Why not?

AMBER: I don't know —

JACK: We don't have to worry about money.

AMBER: It's not the money. It's having a job —

JACK: There's lots of jobs out there. When we get back.

AMBER: Yeah. But I like this one. It's been a challenge. I'm story-boarding my video. I'm going to be able to pay my

	student loan down. And save a bit for a project I want to work on. Just a little indie I want to shoot.

JACK: Well, I could certainly help you out with that.

AMBER: Actually, I'd like to do it myself.

JACK: I wouldn't mind.

AMBER: I don't want your help, OK?

JACK: OK, OK … But what about? You know?

AMBER: What?

JACK: What we have.

AMBER: We spent a little time together. . .

JACK: Two nights.

AMBER: Two nights. Whatever.

JACK: That's all this meant to you? Spending a little time together?

AMBER: No. Not exactly.

JACK: So what's the problem?

AMBER: Well it's just. You know?

JACK: No, I don't know.

AMBER: Well … I'm not trying to be rude or anything or hurt your feelings or anything like that, you know?

JACK: OK …

AMBER: Well it's just that …

JACK: What?

AMBER: You're kinda old? You know?

JACK: Old?

AMBER: Yeah. Kinda.

JACK: Old

AMBER: I'm sorry …

JACK: I see.

AMBER: Like, didn't you tell me you have a daughter who's older than me?

JACK: Yeah …

AMBER: And your wife? What about your wife?

JACK: Well, that's another, you know …

AMBER: No, I don't know.

JACK: Well, we're having a little time out, right now, I guess
          you'd call it —

AMBER: Why? Because of what we did?

JACK: No.

AMBER: Then why?

JACK: It's just, you know, it's a long time to be together, it's a
          long time, it's a … . You know? I don't know.

AMBER: Oh my God. This is what happens, you know, when
          you're not honest? When you lie, and cheat, and carry
          on? This is what happens, Jack. Can't you see that it's
          wrong? That it's no way to live? Can't you see that for
          yourself?

JACK: I don't know.

AMBER: And now you expect me to leave a good job and all the
          plans I have for my career and all my friends and my
          mom and everything and just take off for Asia? With
          you?

JACK: Yeah. Something like that, I guess …

AMBER: Sorry, Jack. It's not going to happen.

JACK: Right. Well, then. I don't know. I don't know … .

          Long pause. AMBER *discreetly checks her watch.*

AMBER: I'm sorry, Jack.

JACK: It's OK.

AMBER: I mean, I'm sorry. I actually have something on tonight.

JACK: Oh?

AMBER: Yeah.

JACK: What?

AMBER: I'm meeting a friend. We're going to this Nine Inch Nails
          tribute thing.

JACK: I see …

AMBER:	And I told my friend I'd meet him there, so I'm going to have to take off pretty soon here. I don't want to be late. I'm sorry.
JACK:	I see.
AMBER:	Yeah.
JACK:	Right. Friends are good. You'll find as you get older that you have fewer and fewer of them. Isn't that odd? It should be the other way around … Is this a friend, or a friend?
AMBER:	I don't know. We haven't figured that out. Actually, you know him.
JACK:	I know your friend?
AMBER:	Yeah.
JACK:	Who?
AMBER:	Johnny.
JACK:	Delvecchio?!
AMBER:	Yeah. He's a big fan of the Nails. So we thought we'd take this thing in tonight. Maybe come back here later for some tea …
JACK:	I see.
AMBER:	So.
JACK:	Yeah.
AMBER:	I should probably get going.
JACK:	Yeah. Me too …
AMBER:	I'll see you sometime?
JACK:	I don't know.
AMBER:	I'll see you around?
JACK:	I doubt it.
AMBER:	Well. Take care.

AMBER leaves the stage.

~

EPILOGUE *OUT OF THE LOOP*

Continuous action. JACK with a putter.

JACK: Not so long ago, I was worried that maybe I was dying. And now, I don't know, now I'm worried that maybe I'm merely meant to live ... endure, somehow ... I don't know .... You know, you get so far out of the loop, you can't get a game with anyone who matters. With anyone. You find yourself golfing with fourteen year olds. And their grandfathers. It's very bad. Very, very bad. Maybe that's the hardest thing, when all is said and done, to be alone. To be left, alone. Always alone.... Anyway. So one day, I was sitting here on this bench, waiting to tee off, waiting for a partner, waiting for someone like me, who didn't have anyone. And she comes walking up from the parking lot. Darlene. You know, even from so far away, I can tell her, by her walk. She kind of does this thing with her neck, when she steps. There's no mistaking her walk. Anyway, up she comes, with a full set of clubs with the little phentex head covers. And a hat with a pom pom. And those legs of hers. And she walks up and looks at me like you'd look at a dog that's done something unfortunate, inappropriate. Whatever. So what can you do? You golf ... you golf. Her short game is atrocious. Absolutely atrocious. And her drives — well, enough said. And I don't believe in my heart that I really deserve it, but I'm glad we're together. Oh yeah, am I ever glad ...

Fade to black.

END OF PLAY

E UGENE STICKLAND is Alberta Theatre
Projects' Playwright in Residence. This is his
fifth play for the *playRites* Festival, beginning with
Some Assembly Required (1994) and continuing with
Sitting on Paradise (1996), *A Guide to Mourning*
(1998) and *Appetite* (2000). His work is produced
frequently in theatres throughout Canada. Eugene
devotes a lot of time and energy to teaching and
mentoring young playwrights — here in Calgary and
as far away as Australia. Eugene lives in North West
Calgary with his wife Carrie and their daughter,
Hannah.

Photograph: Chrystal Cherniwchan Photography
Concept: Bart Habermiller